W9-DDH-456

GEORGIAN COLLEGE LIBRARY

#27.83
GEOB-BK

DISCARD

A **Country Living** BOOK

THE
MOM'S GUIDE
TO RUNNING
A BUSINESS

Strategies for Work Success and Family Balance

MICHELLE LEE RIBEIRO

Library Commons
Georgian College
One Georgian Drive
Barrie, ON
L4M 3X9

HEARST BOOKS
A division of Sterling Publishing Co., Inc.

New York / London
www.sterlingpublishing.com

Copyright © 2011 by Hearst Communications, Inc.
All rights reserved.

Project editor: Carol Spier
Book design: Renato Stanisic
Photography editor: Martha Corcoran

Library of Congress Cataloging-in-Publication Data

Ribeiro, Michelle Lee.
 The mom's guide to running a business : strategies for work success and family balance /
Michelle Lee Ribeiro.
    p. cm.
 At head of title: Country living
 Includes index.
 ISBN 978-1-58816-802-3
1. Work and family—Case studies. 2. Businesswomen—Case studies. 3. Working mothers—
Case studies. 4. Entrepreneurship—Case studies. I. Title. II. Title: Country living.
 HD4904.25.R53 2011
 658.4'09—dc22
                                        201001731

10 9 8 7 6 5 4 3 2 1

Published by Hearst Books
A division of Sterling Publishing Co., Inc.
387 Park Avenue South, New York, NY 10016

Country Living is a registered trademark of Hearst Communications, Inc.

www.countryliving.com

For information about custom editions, special sales, premium and corporate purchases,
please contact Sterling Special Sales Department at 800-805-5489 or
specialsales@sterlingpublishing.com.

Distributed in Canada by Sterling Publishing
c/o Canadian Manda Group, 165 Dufferin Street
Toronto, Ontario, Canada M6K 3H6

Distributed in Australia by Capricorn Link (Australia) Pty. Ltd.
P.O. Box 704, Windsor, NSW 2756 Australia

Manufactured in China

Sterling ISBN 978-1-58816-802-3

Contents ✳

INTRODUCTION **4**

PART 1: PROFILES OF SUCCESS

ARTISANS **8**

SHOP OWNERS AND EVENT PRODUCERS **37**

DESIGNER/PRODUCERS **62**

SERVICE PROVIDERS **124**

PART 2: A BUSINESS MOTHER'S WORKSHOP

THE FIRST STEPS **158**

YOUR BUSINESS PLAN **163**

FINANCING **167**

SPACE AND BOUNDARIES **171**

THE WORK–FAMILY BALANCE **176**

STAYING ON TRACK **180**

RESOURCES **184**

PHOTOGRAPHY CREDITS **190**

INDEX **191**

Introduction

Take a walk downtown and you'll see small businesses everywhere. A few minutes searching the Web for online businesses brings up millions of results. As we shop in those stores and on those sites, we rarely stop to consider the people who own and run them.

IN THIS BOOK YOU'LL MEET SOME OF THE PEOPLE BEHIND THOSE BUSINESSES. And you might be surprised by who they are. The ones who share their stories here are ordinary women who have found a way to make money pursuing a passion. Many of them work at home. All of them have children. And each one of them started out thinking, "There's no way I can do this!" But they did. And so can you.

It doesn't take an MBA to be an entrepreneur, and you don't need a boardroom to make decisions. If you have a hobby, a passion, and a desire to bring your ideas to the world, your creativity can turn a profit. You just need the tools to know how to begin—and the support and inspiration of others who have already done it. In this book, you'll find both.

IN THE FOLLOWING PAGES, 28 MOTHERS SHARE THEIR ENTREPRENEURIAL STORIES: how they started, the challenges they faced, the lessons they've learned along the way. You'll discover how they have balanced the responsibilities and pleasures of business ownership and motherhood. Many of them worried that launching and conducting a business while raising children would be daunting, if not impossible, but they—and their happy children—are all living proof that it can be done. Let their stories be your inspiration and consider their advice the support of many good friends.

TOWARD THE END OF THE BOOK, YOU'LL FIND A WORKSHOP SECTION WITH AN OVERVIEW OF THE BASIC INFORMATION YOU NEED TO KNOW IN ORDER TO RUN A BUSINESS; this covers topics such as business plans and financing. You'll also find chapters devoted specifically to the art of balancing a business and a family, with advice about operating a business out of your home, setting priorities, and finding time to do it all. Let this be your toolbox, equipping you with everything you need to know to move forward with your idea. Use the resources listed at the end to find additional support: informative books, helpful business organizations, and online associations to put you in touch with other entrepreneurs. Also included is a mentor directory, listing the Web site addresses of the profiled women—check these out as models for effective marketing as well as to learn about products that pique your interest.

Yes, starting a business while raising children requires careful planning, commitment, and motivation. But what you'll take away from this book is this: The benefits are worth it. As your own boss, *you* control your days—which means you can be there for your family whenever they need you. The not-so-obvious benefit that the women in this book have discovered? Once the creativity that had been stirring inside of them had a place to live, they were happier, more satisfied, and in turn, better Moms.

If the bravado of these women inspires you to take an entrepreneurial leap, the wisdom they've gained from the bumps in their roads will serve as a parachute. We hope that *your* entrepreneurial endeavor will be a smooth journey, landing you right where you hope to be: with your family, a growing bank account, and a flourishing business.

* 1 *

Profiles of Success

Diane Allison-Stroud

DIANE ALLISON-STROUD:
HANDMADE GAME BOARDS

Boone, North Carolina
dallison.squarespace.com

When Diane Allison-Stroud says she's the kind of person who will "run and jump off a cliff and see what happens," she isn't kidding. In 1994, she was a single, stay-at-home mom—a job she adored—living in Dallas, Texas, with her son, Davey, then 11 years old. One day, she started making game boards on a whim, and found that she could sell them. Two years later, she decided to pack up and move to a small town she'd read about in a book, just to indulge another whim. Today she's happily remarried, the mother of two sons, and swamped with orders for her boards. It's apparent that, in the game of life, Diane likes to roll the dice; so far, she's definitely winning.

✳ BALANCING ACT

"As women and mothers, we're hard on ourselves. We expect to balance many roles and be *perfect* at each one. But it's a balancing act that's always being fine-tuned. Every day is different, and every day something has to give. My mom always says, 'Things will come out in the wash,' and I hold that thought close. I find that to keep my sanity, it's in my best interest to go with the flow."

IT WAS DAVEY'S GROWING INDEPENDENCE THAT GAVE DIANE FREE TIME AND INSPIRED HER TO BEGIN HER BUSINESS. "I noticed that he'd come home from school, drop off his backpack, and head right out to be with his friends," she recalls. "I wasn't needed as a full-time parent anymore, so I began thinking about what course my life could start to take." One day she picked up a magazine that was full of ideas for things to make. She was immediately drawn to the game boards. "They were like miniature quilts on wood, very geometric and colorful," she says. So she gathered paints and brushes, wood, nails, and a small saw and started creating. It was a hobby at first, but then her friends gave her an idea: Why not try to sell the boards? She wrote a letter describing her product, took a few snapshots of some of her creations, and sent them out to a list of stores she'd found in the back of *Country Living* magazine. Before she knew it, she was slammed with orders—and her hobby turned into a full-blown business.

Things went well, and Diane decided to shake things up once again. She loved her friends in Dallas but decided she wanted to move her son to a small, safer town, a place she considered "a beautiful spot of paradise." She picked up a book called *Best Small Towns in America* and decided on Boone, North Carolina. "I packed up our little Corolla with our five cats and headed out," she says. It was there that she met her current husband and later gave birth to their son, Eli. "It's funny how things work out,"

Opposite and page 9: Diane's game boards are whimsical, vividly colored, and very graphic, in the tradition of folk examples that inspire them.

Right: Prior to painting, Diane draws a design on a bare, precut board. **Right, below:** A close look reveals the nuanced hand of the artist.

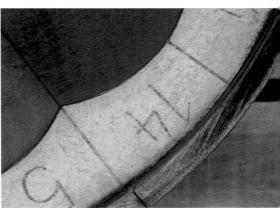

she reflects. "I love to tell my husband that's why I came here—because he was here waiting for me."

With a successful business, a teenage son, and a toddler, the juggling began. Davey was in school all day, and busy with friends and after-school activities in the afternoons. But Eli was home with Diane. She was working out of a studio in her home, so she set him up right beside her. "He'd have a paintbrush in one hand and wood in the other, creating his own art," she says. When Davey was home, he'd help out by packing and carrying boxes. At this time, Diane was working 12 hours a day, every day, and everything was scheduled around her family. When the days were packed with family commitments, she'd work in the

✳**OH NO THEY DIDN'T!** "At one point, I enrolled my younger son, Eli, in preschool a few mornings a week so he could make friends and have some fun. I went to a parent–teacher conference and was told that Eli didn't know his colors too well. I was confused, because I knew he'd known his colors for years—he always 'pulled' colors for me when I was working. So when I got home, I set out a bunch of paints and asked him what colors they were. He stated clearly: 'Barn red, orange marmalade, eggplant.' I assured myself he was just fine!"

✳HOW THE KIDS SEE IT "I remember growing up and helping my mom out with stuff—like sanding, waxing, and buffing boards. It was fun. But I will say I was embarrassed when she'd pick me up from school wearing overalls covered in paint!"

—**Davey, 25**

Above: Diane's son Davey, in the middle, looks on as her husband and their son Eli share a lighthearted moment.

Opposite: Diane's spacious studio includes an area for painting and another with open racks on which the boards can dry.

middle of the night, often painting at 2 a.m. She employed local college students to help out with her business—and sometimes her kids.

"I WANTED THE BEST OF BOTH WORLDS—TO HAVE A BUSINESS AND RAISE MY KIDS WITHOUT DAY CARE," DIANE SAYS. "I was lucky that there was a college in town with a lot of aspiring artists. Not only would they work for my business, they'd also pitch in with anything I needed, whether it was building boats out of leaves and sticks for Eli or starting supper. They really were like daughters to me." Her kids, she says, weren't lacking attention. If anything fell by the wayside, it was time alone for her and her husband. "Hubby, I think, should get an award," she says lovingly of his patience. But both of them are enjoying the present. "My husband and I know we have the rest of our lives to do whatever we want, whenever we want—and believe me, we have big plans! But right now, we love just being a family together, playing games, going to the movies, or going to the park."

Now that Davey is 25 and Eli is 9, Diane finds it much easier to manage everything. With Eli at

school, she can focus on her boards all day without a toddler in her lap. While she and her husband look forward to their big plans, they're not hurrying the future along. "One day, I know we'll be saddened that the house is too clean, and everything's too organized," she says. "We'd rather have our kids in the home. But I know my kids will be out there practicing what they grew up around. They won't be scared to leap off a cliff and see what happens. They'll achieve success and tell me all about it. And of course, I hope they'll take time out to play on these game boards I make—or else life just wouldn't be fair."

✳**JUST ROLL WITH IT** "Sometimes I feel like I get whiplash jumping back and forth during the day—in my 'work zone' one minute, then all of a sudden it's carpool time. But I just take it as it comes. If I hit a hurdle down the road, I'll figure out a way to overcome it. If you actually think about all the problems that could arise, you'll scare yourself into not trying."

Ann Marie Craig

CENTURY FARMHOUSE:
HANDCRAFTED ARTISAN SOAPS

West Bend, Wisconsin
centuryfarmhouse.com

Ann Marie Craig has fond childhood memories of watching her grandmother make soap at home as a matter of course. Years later, living in the same farmhouse with her own family, she taught herself to do the same—as a hobby that soon became something more. "My house was filling up with soap. I knew I had to start selling it," says Ann Marie. All of a sudden, she was running a manufacturing business out of the kitchen. "There were times when I couldn't find a chair to sit on among all the soap," remembers Ann Marie's daughter Emily, who was 18 at the time. Emily's memories are lighthearted, but the truth is that she and her sisters—Erin, then 20, and Madeleine, then 3—were living in something of a soap factory.

WHEN YOU'RE RAISING A FAMILY WHILE LAUNCHING A BUSINESS FROM HOME, THE LINE BETWEEN PERSONAL AND WORK TENDS TO GET BLURRY. No one knows this more than Ann Marie. Her home, a generations-old farmhouse, doubles as a soap-making factory and was also the inspiration for her company name: Century Farmhouse. The soaps are made from natural ingredients—rainwater, snow, lavender, maple sap—that she collects herself or purchases from local farmers. Everything is done on the premises. She mixes the soaps on her kitchen stove and lets the molds dry on her front porch. Then they sit in a spare bedroom upstairs to cure for a few weeks. This environment is something that

Below: A rapt audience watches Ann Marie make soap at the Country Living Fair. At the front of the table are fresh herbs, waiting to be chopped and stirred into the pot.

✳BALANCING ACT

"It can sometimes feel like there's a constant struggle to keep everything running smoothly at both work and home, but there's one basic rule: Family needs to come first. Of course there are times when one or the other needs more attention, but don't let the needs of the job override the home on a regular basis. Because if things aren't working well at home, it's very hard to concentrate on the job."

✳**PITFALLS & TRIUMPHS** "I constantly find myself having to correct the misconception among people—including my own family—that soap-making is a 'nice little hobby.' Shortly after I started making soap, my father handed me a 20-dollar bill and told me to go buy some soap! Now he's one of my staunchest supporters."

the older girls had to learn to get used to. Their mom had been a nurse and a part-time teacher for most of their lives when she suddenly became a home-based entrepreneur. Emily and Erin were old enough that they weren't physically there to be affected by it all the time, but it was still overwhelming.

While space has always been an issue, Ann Marie was lucky not to struggle too much with scheduling. With her two older daughters quite independent, she only had to worry about Madeleine. She only mixed soap when Maddie was at school, to make sure her youngest girl was never anywhere around the lye. The rest of it just fell into place. "Making and packaging the soap didn't take up the whole day, so there was always time for kids' stuff: laundry and other things," says Ann Marie. "Then I'd focus on the office work in the afternoon, when Maddie was home."

BOTH OLDER GIRLS TOOK AN INTER-EST IN THE SELLING ASPECT OF THE BUSINESS. Ann Marie sees that as a bonus. "I never really expected my children to work for my business," she says. "Their willingness to help out has helped create a bond of accomplishment between us. I don't expect them

Opposite: Ann Marie greases a large soap mold. Once firm, the soap block will be forced through the blue-framed wire grid cutter, to be cut first into long bricks, and then into small pieces.

Above: Century Farmhouse soaps are lovely to look at and often fragrant. From the top are Malvina's Wish (a soap for love and luck made with white heather), Lavender Luffa Spa soap, and Maple Sap Vanilla soap.

to continue to work with me indefinitely. If they want to do so, though, I'd welcome them!" Rather than try to bring her kids into the business, she focuses on getting them excited about family time, and making sure it doesn't fall to the wayside. "Being there for family holidays and keeping the family traditions going are really important to me," she says. "I try to involve Maddie in simple things like meal planning and cookie baking, so she feels she can take a greater role in the family goings-on. I think it makes the few times that I'm not available for activities less of an issue."

SUCCESS PRESENTS ANN MARIE WITH AN EMOTIONAL HURDLE: THE BUSINESS HAS OUTGROWN THE FARMHOUSE IT WAS NAMED FOR. Little by little, her principal sales outlet of local

---

✳**HOW THE KIDS SEE IT** "Every year in October, the beginning of the Christmas selling season, Mom begins her late-night soap-wrapping sessions. To entertain herself and her helpers, she cycles through two of her favorite Christmas movies—over, and over, and over again. By December, Bing Crosby is in my nightmares."

—Erin, 28

---

farmers' markets expanded to include limited wholesaling. Her business doubled when she started accepting orders from all over through her Web site. Living among endless bars of soap has been inconvenient, to say the least, and Ann Marie says it's now time to move on by moving out. "The business has grown to the point that a move is necessary for both business growth and family sanity," she says. "But the story of Century Farmhouse is so inextricably linked to the house in which I live, it's a little tricky to move it to another location, in terms of marketing. I'm working on how I can be as faithful as possible to the story of the soaps and the farmhouse venue." Ann Marie is ready to take the leap.

Opposite: Ann Marie's daughters Madeleine, Emily, and Erin have cheerfully lived among bars of soap for years.

Right: Ann Marie stands in the doorway of her family farmhouse, freshly made soaps in hand.

✳**DOSES OF REALITY** "My children ground me. It's hard to think too highly of yourself with a sick child needing you in the middle of the night. Then you're just Mommy, and all the business ups and downs are rather meaningless. There is more to life than the business you create, and my children remind me of that daily."

Jennifer List and Stacy Waddington

SEVEN SMOOCHES: ONE-OF-A-KIND CHILDREN'S CLOTHING AND ACCESSORIES

Flossmoor, Illinois
sevensmooches.com

One mom caring full-time for five kids and another with two kids and a job aren't in the ideal situation for an entrepreneurial endeavor. But friends Jennifer List (on the left) and Stacy Waddington made it work. While raising their children—and with no employees but themselves—Jennifer and Stacy found time to create a line of children's clothing and accessories called Seven Smooches (named for the love of their seven little ones). They agree that it wouldn't have been possible without two very supportive husbands and their tight-knit partnership. These ladies prove that when you have someone to lean on, nothing is impossible.

☀BALANCING ACT

"Scheduling can get tricky. We'd always like more time with our spouses. After the first year, we learned where we could carve out a little more personal time, and what is a nice-to-do versus a need-to-do for the business. The important thing is to make sure our families know that even when we're busy, if they need us, they can always count on Mom being there."

Above: Tiny, adorable bunny slippers with hand-embroidered faces and carrot appliqués on the soles show the Seven Smooches' pitch-perfect attention to detail.

IT ALL STARTED OUT IN A PRESCHOOL IN ILLINOIS. Jennifer and Stacy had kids in the same class, and the women met as volunteer room mothers, leading crafts projects. They discovered they both had design backgrounds and a taste for the same aesthetic, and began to talk about starting a business together. "Stacy was a visual merchandising manager for the Gap and had been looking for a way to leave corporate retail," says Jennifer, who was a busy stay-at-home mother of five. "And I was ready to do something creative. We decided it might be nice to try to show our work to an audience beyond preschool."

In 2007, they decided on a concept: They'd create kids' clothes and accessories from recycled materials, like old wool sweaters and flour sacks. They'd sew it all themselves during the day, while their kids were in school, and market it at trade shows. And they'd do it all right in their homes. Jennifer volunteered her

front room and dining room to be the main workspace; Stacy devoted a small corner of her bedroom to the business. After showing at a few trade shows and sending freebies to celebrity moms for publicity, the business took off. Now they sell their wares online, in catalogs, and wholesale to stores.

"HONESTLY, WE COULDN'T DO THIS WITHOUT THE UNFAILING HELP OF FRIENDS AND FAMILY," says Jennifer. Operating a business like theirs without employees is time consuming and stressful, but Jennifer and Stacy are lucky: They have each other—and very helpful husbands, parents, and friends. Their girlfriends pitch in with the sewing when they receive a giant order. And when they have to travel, their families take care of the kids. "Even after a long day at work, our husbands will play with our kids and keep them occupied whenever we have to sew. And our mothers are there to help with anything we need—baby-sitting, cutting, sewing, cooking, laundry . . ." Luckily, their hubbies are also good

✳PITFALLS & TRIUMPHS "When we travel for work, we put our collection in our carry-on luggage, but everything else—the display for the show, marketing materials, order forms, etc.—has to be checked. One time, Stacy also checked 40 handmade cardigans she was bringing to a client. The luggage did not make it onto the plane. It was very scary, to say the least. Fortunately, it arrived at 4:30 a.m. the next day, just in time for the show."

Above: This pink bird is just one of Jen and Stacy's charming felted accessories.

Right and page 20: Blanket-stitched edges, witty embroidery, and oversize buttons add to the fun of felted, recycled, graphic fabrics.

✳**HOW THE KIDS SEE IT** "Yeah, my mom is always busy. But there's always something that could be worse—at least she's at *home* working. Plus, I help out, cutting labels and giving my opinion. And I help sort sweaters into color piles."

—Stacy's daughter, Stella, 12

sports. "I would be lying if I said we've never accidentally felted one of our husband's sweaters," Jennifer admits.

Getting their kids to accept that Mom is busy when she's at home has been the biggest conflict they've faced. "We sew in the car at baseball practice, while watching soccer games, and at Irish dancing class," Jennifer explains. Stacy's kids were used to her leaving the house for work, so when she suddenly had to work at home, they were frustrated. And Jennifer's kids had a hard time understanding that while she was home as usual, she was no longer able to spend all her time with them. "Kids are incredibly resilient and flexible and forgiving, but they still have trouble understanding deadlines," says Jennifer. "I have to help them understand why I can't take them somewhere as quickly as I might have been able to before the business. I gently remind them that Mom needs to do fun things too, and that sewing is fun for me. That—and a strategically placed ice cream trip—seem to do the trick."

Both women have included their children in the business, as a way to help them understand it more. All the kids model clothes for photo shoots, test out sweaters and report back on the "itchiness factor," and help out cutting labels and pinning tags. "They love telling us when they like something," says Jennifer. "They'll say, 'Ooh, that sweater is so great!' And we know it's a winner." Jennifer has perhaps only one regret about how she's balanced her business and family. "Maybe we should have taught the older kids to sew," she jokes. "Then they could have helped out more during crunch times."

THROUGH IT ALL, HAVING A PARTNER— IN BUSINESS AND IN FRIENDSHIP—HAS BEEN KEY TO HELPING THEM BOTH STAY SANE. While Stacy went to New York for their second trade show, Jennifer was in Europe with her family. She was able to take the vacation because Stacy offered to travel to the show alone. And on a daily basis, the two women pick up little treats for each other to get them through tough times. "We buy each other books we know the other will like, or even just a Starbucks coffee for a minute of peace," says Jennifer.

Opposite: The "seven smooches" are Annika List, Mason List, Jasper Waddington, Noah List, Eli List, Greta List, and Stella Waddington.

Above: Jen's youngest, Mason, puts thought into a "birthday cake" he's making for Mommy.

☀**LEAN ON ME** "Stacy and I balance each other quite well. We are excellent at talking each other down during stressful times, and only one of us is allowed to be 'on the edge' at a time. We remind each other that the end always does justify the means—even if the 'end' is simply a really pretty cardigan with the most perfect buttons!"

Betz White

BETZ WHITE PRODUCTIONS:
FELTED HOME AND BABY ACCESSORIES

Maryland
betzwhite.com

In her thirties, married with two young children, Betz White made the decision to leave the corporate world and continue her apparel design career as a freelancer, from home, so she could work less and have more time to spend with her sons. She picked up an old hobby—felting—and began converting thrift-store sweaters into new items like pillows, journals, and baby blankets. Things went well and she enjoyed being with her kids, but now she craved adult contact. So in 2005, she exhibited her creations at a craft fair in order to meet some fellow crafters. People loved her work and her life quickly took a new turn. Now she has her own design company and has written two books. Looks like that "work less" plan didn't work out so well!

"On occasion, I'll opt out of joining a family excursion so I can get some extra work done. But I'm around for all the little daily stuff and normal family routines. I'm home after their school day, I'm there to help them with homework, and I'm there to make dinner. Of course, there's an ebb and flow throughout the year, but as long as we remain adaptable we're able to find a balance."

WHEN HER FELTED CREATIONS WERE SO WELL RECEIVED AT THAT CRAFT FAIR, BETZ STARTED MAKING MORE OF THEM. Her husband created a Web site for her. Betz set up a selling account on Etsy, an e-commerce site devoted to handmade products. When she launched Betz White Productions, she says, "I had no big-picture plan. I just knew I had to start somewhere, and I already had the sewing machine and a computer. I found a bank that offered very low-cost business banking, and I went for it."

At the time, Sean was 3 and Conner was 5, so they required a lot of attention. Betz carefully carved out time for work, and time for them. "I had 'Mommy Days' when they were at home, and 'Work Days' when they were at preschool," she explains. "I had to be very disciplined to get a much done as possible on Work Days so that I could give the kids my full attention on Mommy Days." She has been

Above: A large design board mounted on one wall of her studio gives Betz ample room to keep visual inspiration and plans for new work in view.

Right: To give small, classic fabric accessories like eyeglass cases and wallets a fresh finish, Betz trims them with posy shapes she cuts out and arranges in layers.

Above and below: Says Betz of the thrift store sweaters she turns into whimsical cupcakes, "If one is a color you'd eat, I will buy it."

Above right: Intricate felt cutouts grace pillows made with bold swaths of color.

Right: Cocoa anyone? Betz's sweater mugfuls are topped with felt whipped cream.

able to squeeze in work on Mommy Days too. Her office—a spare bedroom in her home—overlooks her backyard and the neighborhood park, so she can both work and keep an eye on the kids when they're outside playing.

For Betz, who grew up in a crafty family, keeping a carefully planned schedule is where the business–family separation ends. Her mother encouraged her creativity and taught her to knit at an early age, and her grandmother urged her to attend design school after college. Betz credits them both as mentors. Continuing the tradition, she has a couch in her office that's strewn with pillows and books, where her kids are welcome to flop down and work on their own craft projects.

Above: Cute, colorful little birds are fun gifts. The ones in back can be used as pincushions, the one in front is a zippered pouch.

Right: Betz transforms bright stripes—plain and patterned—into cheery Christmas stockings, complete with decorative stitches and trimmed cuffs.

❋**OH NO THEY DIDN'T!**

"In 2008, I participated in a craft fair in Virginia. At the last minute our childcare fell through so we had to bring the boys with us. I brought a small folding table and some art supplies so they could draw pictures and occupy themselves without getting in the way. Well, the entrepreneurial spirit rubbed off on them: After a few hours of getting compliments from people, they made a sign and started selling their artwork for 25 cents a piece!"

Above: True to family tradition, Betz's two sons are already crafty: Sean sews, and Conner creates spool-knitted cord.

Opposite: A computer, a worktable, and a sewing machine are all key to Betz's work; they're all easily accessed in her studio.

IT'S HER KIDS SHE TURNS TO WHEN SHE WANTS A TRUE, NO-HOLDS-BARRED OPINION OF HER MERCHANDISE. "My younger son, who's now 7, has an eye for design and a clear idea in his head about how something should look," she says. "He's actually a great sounding board when I just need a pure from-the-gut design opinion." More than that, they are a constant reminder of what it takes to be a great designer. As Betz explains it, "They've taught me that putting potato chips in your sandwich tastes good—try something unexpected! It's not as fun if you don't get dirty, so lighten up; everything doesn't have to be perfect! And the world looks different when you hang upside down—try looking at things with a new perspective! These are great lessons that apply to parenting, business, and life in general."

✳**HOW THE KIDS SEE IT** "The only thing that annoys me about my mom's work is the sewing machine. That thing is noisy!"

—Sean, 7

"I help out my mom sometimes by crank-knitting i-cord. I do it to earn money for Legos."

—Conner, 9

✳**JUST MAKE IT WORK** "You can't let obstacles overpower you. I had a big craft show in 2006 and two days before we were leaving, my business cards showed up with a typo. My parents had come to town to baby-sit while my husband and I were away, and we sat at the kitchen table and trimmed 1,000 cards to remove the misprint. So I ended up with mini cards at the show, but it was a success anyway."

Meredith Clark

CHANDI DESIGN: ONE-OF-A-KIND CHANDELIERS AND SCONCES

Los Angeles, California
chandidesign.com

When Meredith Clark started making chandeliers, she cradled her infant son, Dante, against her chest in a sling while hand-beading her intricate creations. More than ten years later, her company, Chandi Design, is thriving. Meredith produces both wholesale and custom-made creations from her home studio, and with Dante and his younger brother, Zane, around, things can get pretty crazy. Meredith finds that the stress can always be managed—with a little bit of laughter.

MEREDITH STUMBLED INTO CHANDELIER MAKING; SHE HAD ORIGINALLY PLANNED A CAREER IN ALTERNATIVE MEDICINE. But in 1997, when her then-husband, a buyer for Shabby Chic, was unable to find "the perfect lighting" in his forays through flea markets, she volunteered to take a stab at making a chandelier for his company. She set up at a living room table, stringing exquisite beads she had collected over time, and created her first piece. Her biggest challenge wasn't keeping Dante occupied but keeping him close to her: Meredith practices attachment parenting, a nurturing philosophy that includes lots of physical contact between parents and babies. The sling provided the answer, and she got to work. "I learned how to work with my arms outstretched, just out of his reach, because he was always trying to get his hands on the materials," she remembers.

By the time Zane was born a couple of years later, Chandi was in full swing, with a number of wholesale clients, including Shabby Chic and Meredith's sister-in-law's company, Shade. In her studio, Meredith kept the boys amused with crystals strung as a mobile. When she went bead shopping, she took the boys with her. "I would create games of I Spy to keep them happy in stores. I remember the looks of horror I would get as we walked into rooms filled with delicate strands of beads and crystals—it was apparent the merchants were terrified of the boys causing an accident." Dante and Zane left the stores intact, but Meredith admits that there were a

✴**BALANCING ACT**

"Laughter brings me balance. It is the shared moments of absurdity that allow my many lives to coexist. How many people get to experience a single moment in their home as I do—drawing a new light into being while another me is walking a client through crystal colors on the phone and another me is perfecting a leafed finish in the studio, all while a boy is mooning me from the kitchen window?"

few accidents at home. "Most of my materials were of choking size, so it was crucial that I keep it all out of my boys' reach. Fortunately, we made it through without any disasters—but there were diaper changes that gave me a sparkling surprise."

CHANDI HAS A SMALL STAFF, AND WHILE THEY HAVE BECOME LIKE PART OF THE FAMILY, Meredith says that the separation of professional from personal time and space in her home studio has posed a bit of a problem as her boys have gotten older and more mischievous. They vie for her attention when they're at home and sometimes annoy her assistants by leaving candy wrappers on their desks or snatching water coolers away to fill them with Kool-Aid. Meredith tries to combat their frustrations by being clear and communicative about what she needs to do on the drive home from school, mapping out the afternoon and evening and explaining how much work she has left to do and when she'll be free to hang out with them.

When the studio workday ends, usually around 5 or 5:30, Meredith quickly transforms the space back into a home, leaving no evidence of Chandi to remind her of work. She also plans

✳OH NO THEY DIDN'T!

"Zane has always had a fascination with those packing peanuts. When he was about 3 years old, he was in the studio at my house and I ran upstairs for a minute. When I got back, I discovered him completely immersed in a bag of peanuts, only his giggling face peeking out through the hole through which he had climbed. Whenever I do shows now, I take a moment to jump into an empty crate of peanuts and send him a picture of my smiling, floating head."

✳**HOW THE KIDS SEE IT** "Last week, my friends and I were talking about what our moms do. One of my friends said, 'Dante's mom makes chandeliers—and they're badass!' My other friend said, 'Yeah, she can make turds look like platinum!' I thought: my mom is awesome! I'm glad my mom is mine."

—Dante, 13

"adventure Fridays" every once in a while, when she forgoes work to have a special long weekend with her kids. "We go to a museum, for a hike, to the beach," she says. "We don't return home until the last signs of Chandi are gone for the week."

MEREDITH RELIES ON UTTER GOOFI-NESS TO SOOTHE FRUSTRATIONS AND CONFLICTS AMONG STAFF AND FAMILY. "There are moments when the air is palpable with tension between me and the boys, or one of my colleagues and the boys," she says. "That's when I put on music and dance. My particular favorite of late is *Where Is the Love?* by the Black Eyed Peas and Justin Timberlake. It's so not my style that you can't

Opposite: When lighted, chandeliers like Globe, a sphere of crystal beads, appear magical from all angles.

Right: Meredith's sons, Dante, top, and Zane, have outgrown the prank stage and are now two of her biggest fans.

Above: The chandeliers are temporarily hung for easy assembly. Here Meredith, assisted by a colleague, wires beads to a metal canopy.

help but giggle when you see me ridiculously jumping around to that song." Another stress-relieving tactic she uses is the run around the block. When someone's getting a little tense, they're sent for a jog. "It's never received well by the boys, but they admit they always return happier," she says.

When Meredith travels for trade shows, her sons stay with her ex-husband. While she's happy they have the time with him, she misses them immensely when she's gone for more than a few days. "The first time I left them for a week, even though I knew they were in good hands, the separation anxiety I felt was one of the most powerful feelings I have known," says Meredith. "But they enjoy those times without me because they get some concentrated time with their dad." It may be that separation anxiety that's preventing Meredith from moving her business out of her home. She says she knows it's time—Chandi really has outgrown the current space—but she isn't ready to make the move quite yet. "We are all starting to feel the pinch, and I do think we're just about ready for that shift," she says of finding commercial space. "But every time I have thought about it, I've changed my mind. I know we all have to leave the nest sometime, but I like my world."

✳**HAVE AN AGENDA** "I have Monday meetings with my staff where we talk about everything we need to get done that week—and I include Mom duties. We talk about what parts need to be ordered, what follow-up with clients needs to happen, what frames need to be drawn, and what specific Mom obligations need to be worked into our schedule. When those meetings don't happen, the week inevitably flows less smoothly."

Heidi Chapman

THE CLOVERLEAF: FUN AND ECLECTIC ANTIQUES AND FASHIONS

Ardmore, Oklahoma
thecloverleafboutique.com

Now in college, Heidi Chapman's son, Jackson, has fond memories of the early days of his mother's business. Wandering through her fledgling shop in Ardmore, Oklahoma, the then-teenager came across giant pink birds, "old food," and, um, proctology devices. The bonus? Plenty of young female staffers to keep him occupied. Flash forward nearly ten years and his mother's shop has evolved into a thriving business, with Cloverleaf boutiques in a total of three cities

selling everything from eclectic fashions to unique gift items. Of course, if you find yourself needing a 15'-tall ice cream cone, they have that too.

✳**BALANCING ACT** "I have no secrets—I just did my best by the seat of my pants. My son was a teenager, so he didn't need me as much as a younger child would have. I made time to attend his school events and golf tournaments, and our home became a gathering spot for his friends. We were probably the only family in town that had a weekly poker game where the mode of transportation was a bicycle!"

HEIDI CHAPMAN HAD ALWAYS PLANNED TO
WORK IN RETAIL. In the early 1980s, she did
exactly that, opening a gift store in her native
Oklahoma City. But after a number of bank
failures and the demise of the oil industry in
her state, she was forced to close up shop. She
returned to school for a master's degree and
went to work in the mental health field. After
15 years, she found herself itching to get back
to the retail world, and in the spring of 2000,
she approached her husband about opening a
shop and found him to be extremely supportive. Luckily, he was in a position to help her
out financially, and Heidi found a space nearby
their home. They purchased it, and the Cloverleaf opened for business.

**"I HIT THE GROUND RUNNING AND NEVER
LOOKED BACK,"** says Heidi. At first, she filled
the space with outside vendors, creating a sort
of antiques mall so she could collect rent to
finance her business. Vendors would show up
with all sorts of strange merchandise—like the
above-mentioned medical tools and weird stale
food. Soon Heidi decided to go it alone and
filled the space with her own merchandise. She
scoured the country for unique finds, purchasing
items that piqued her interest. "Starting a business takes you away from your family more than
average, and I always felt—and still feel—a little
guilt," she confesses. Her husband seemed to roll
with her long hours, the travel required for stock-
ing the shop, and even the huge ice cream cone

Opposite: Eclecticism rules at the
Cloverleaf boutique, where a quirky
assortment of home and fashion
accessories has undeniable allure.

Top: While waiting for a new home,
this pink porch glider makes a fine
background for large sign letters.

Above: The chance to discover a
treasure like this "pearl"-encrusted
boot draws shoppers to the Cloverleaf.

✳**HOW THE KIDS SEE IT** "The biggest benefit for me had to be the array of young ladies cycling in and out of employment. As far as 'helping out' with the business, I'd occasionally lift heavy things. I believe in the separation of church and state—the less I get involved, the less chance there is of jeopardizing my relationship with my mother. So I keep my distance!"

—Jackson, 22

Heidi "knew I had to have, " but she was concerned—especially when it came to her son. "I was always a little worried he would suffer," she says.

HEIDI FOUND CREATIVE WAYS TO KEEP JACKSON INVOLVED WITH HER LIFE. She made sure to schedule "family night" every Thursday at the local country club. But Jackson was a young teenager—a time when most boys are ready to spread their wings. "Most of the time he'd opt to go play golf instead," says Heidi. So she tried a new tactic: hiring young women to work in her shop. "I employed a lot of teenage girls his age, including his girlfriend, so it was a fun place to hang out," she says. "Jackson was there a lot! Plus, I always heard all of the gossip and everything that was going on at school, so he couldn't get away with a thing."

All in all, Heidi believes everything worked out very well. Jackson's now in college, and he couldn't be more well-adjusted. "He didn't turn

Opposite: They don't do this every day, but Heidi, in the bouffant wig, and her staff are in no way afraid to get fully into the spirit of the Cloverleaf boutique.

Above: Relaxed and grinning, Heidi's son Jackson takes his mother's business in stride.

into a serial killer or anything!" jokes Heidi. "He's a very creative soul, very bohemian and free-spirited. And he loves to cook and is great at it—maybe because he was deprived of home-cooked meals!"

✳**SWEET SUCCESS** "I knew I had made it when someone in Texas told me they'd heard of my store. It made me want to do one of those arm pumps and say, '*Yes!*' But my son told me never to do that again after I did it at one of his golf tournaments—so I'll refrain!"

Debbie Haupt

HAUPT ANTIEK MARKET: MONTHLY ANTIQUES MARKET

Apple Valley, Minnesota
hauptantiek.com

Debbie Haupt has always had an entrepreneurial spirit, and working from home is not new to her. For 10 years, she ran a day care program at her house. Later, she started a small business selling banners for baby showers and school spirit items. Then she shifted gears again and began working on a wedding decoration business. But it was her lifelong passion for antiquing that stuck. After amassing far more treasures than she could use, she found she could fund her obsession, be around for her son and two daughters, and get rid of the surplus by selling antiques for a profit—from her garage.

FOR MUCH OF HER LIFE, ANTIQUING WAS JUST A HOBBY; DEBBIE MADE MONEY FROM HER OTHER BUSINESSES. Then, one day in 1997—while in the midst of launching her wedding decor business—she attended an estate sale with a friend. She found numerous things she loved and bought far too many of them. "I've always loved a good bargain, and I found way more things than I needed to decorate our home," she remembers. "I decided to sell the extras out of our garage." That's when something clicked: Antiquing could be her work. Why not turn her garage sale into a regular event?

Debbie dropped her other endeavors and turned her hobby into her job. She hunted for treasures for months, just as she'd always done, and then, to begin her new business, opened up her garage as a shop three times a year. Debbie discovered this was a perfect way to make some money while not having to venture far afield. In 2003, she made a more serious commitment: She obtained commercial space so she could rent booths to other vendors, and under the name Haupt Antiek Market, she started holding weekend-long antiques sales every month.

Not many people would have the nerve to take such a leap. But to Debbie it wasn't so scary. She credits her parents with giving her

Above: Because Haupt Antiek Market is open only once a month, Debbie posts the next sale date outside the shop.

Right: Debbie, often accompanied by her entire family, shops in Europe as well as around the States to find appealing merchandise like these old drawers.

✳**BALANCING ACT**

"We do our paperwork at home. We have an 'office,' but I prefer to work in the family room, since it's closer to the coffee maker—and wine! I tend to fill the kitchen table with papers, which I then have to clear into piles whenever it's time to eat."

such an adventurous spirit. "When I was a kid, my parents saved up to take a year off, and we traveled around the country in a trailer, camping our way through 45 states," she recalls. "They taught me it's okay to take a risk, to live outside of the norm. It was a wonderful adventure." Her parents love the idea of Haupt Antiek, and help out by sweeping up, bringing meals, and hanging signs.

BECAUSE THE SHOP WAS ONLY OPEN ONCE A MONTH, FINDING TIME FOR HER KIDS ON A DAILY BASIS WASN'T AN ISSUE FOR DEBBIE. They were already 14, 11, and 9 when she started, so they spent a lot of time at school and after-school activities. If they needed her they knew where she'd be: in the garage, prepping pieces to move to the commercial space come show time. "We haven't parked a car in the garage in 12 years!" she notes. Her kids, in fact, have been a huge asset. All of them have helped move her wares from the garage to the shop for sales. And now that they're older, their unique interests are turning out to be helpful as well. One of her daughters is an avid photographer, and shoots the business's annual mailing card photos.

All in all, Debbie says the business has been a great way for her to work and

---

✳**HOW THE KIDS SEE IT** "I've always felt really fortunate to have the family business. It was a good option for earning money—it's much more relaxing to do paperwork for my parents in my pajamas than to go out and do a real job!"

—Kristy, 26

✳ OH NO THEY DIDN'T!

"During sale weekends, I often miss meals. My husband cooks—he's really always done the cooking, even before I started Haupt Antiek. In fact, when my daughter Ali was in preschool, I remember asking her if she played 'house' at school one day. She said yes. I then asked her if she got to pretend to cook dinner, and she said, 'No, someone else was the dad!'"

be around her family every day. The only downside? It may have turned her children off to the very thing she's so passionate about. "My younger daughter wanted to decorate her room with pressed wood shelving from Target," she says with a note of disdain. "I think my kids have hauled too much stuff for me to be in love with antiques at all."

Opposite: An old bowl and silver-plated pitcher, "styled" for one of Debbie's sales.

Below: While moving the business into a new, larger space, the Haupt family takes a break from shopping, unpacking, and displaying antiques.

✳ DON'T FORGET THE FUN "My vendors and I like to do funny things during busy sales. My favorite is to put high prices on very ugly things to see if anyone notices."

Serena Thompson

THE FARM CHICKS ANTIQUES SHOW/ HOME ACCESSORIES

Spokane, Washington
thefarmchicks.com

Being a stay-at-home mom to four young children is a hefty job on its own. But that didn't stop Serena Thompson from forging ahead with her dream to start an antiques show in her hometown. In 2002, she partnered with a friend, Teri Edwards (who has since retired from the business), and launched the first Farm Chicks Antiques Show in a friend's barn. As the event grew to an annual show with 150 vendors and the Farm Chicks began contributing style and food stories to *Country Living* magazine, Serena was juggling changing diapers, hunting for antiques, developing products and crafts for her business, and tending to the occasional family emergency. Business and family have thrived—her secret is a positive attitude that allows her to handle anything with a smile.

IT COULD BE SERENA'S UPBRINGING THAT GAVE HER THE FLEXIBILITY TO RAISE FOUR KIDS WHILE CREATING A SUCCESSFUL BUSINESS out of a passion for junk. When she was a child, her best friend was named Shotgun. Her family also hung around folks named Mountain Mike, Snake, and Cat, all very normal to a girl who grew up traveling around the U.S., Mexico, and Canada in a "hippie gypsy wagon" her father built himself. Serena spent her days searching for arrowheads and living without running water or electricity. It was through that lifestyle that she learned to appreciate unique finds and make do with what's there.

As an adult, Serena continued to be charmed by vintage and handmade goods and took an interest in antiques shows. She and Teri loved discovering old stuff, and soon had more than they could use. They decided to hold a sale in a friend's barn, and they did it

✳BALANCING ACT

"There have been many occasions when I was on an important business call and my children could be heard in the background. It's not ideal, but I have always made sure that everyone I work with knows I'm a stay-at-home mom. And if they don't accept that, then they're not right for me. I'll never be able to go back and make up lost time with my family, so they are my priority."

Above: For several years , until it outgrew the grange and town green, the annual Farm Chicks show took over the small town of Fairfield, WA.

✳**OH NO THEY DIDN'T!** "Of course, trying to work with three kids in diapers at home, things happened. One morning when I was rushing to get my oldest son ready for school, one of the younger boys needed a diaper change, and the other two were sitting next to me on the floor. I changed the messy diaper, set it aside, and was putting a clean one on. I glanced over at the other two boys to discover that one of them was eating the contents of the old diaper. I called our pediatrician in a panic, thinking for sure he was going to get some sort of horrible sickness. But she calmly told me this happens all the time and he'd be fine. And he was."

in style, advertising themselves—the producers—as the Farm Chicks. Now the Farm Chicks Antiques Show is an annual event that draws visitors from all over the country to the Spokane Expo Center, Serena is a contributing editor to *Country Living*, and the Farm Chicks have published two books.

GETTING TO THIS POINT WAS NOT AN EASY FEAT, BUT IT HAS BEEN EXCITING. When Serena began, her kids were 10, 3, 2, and 1—all but the oldest in diapers and home with her all day. "My computer was in my laundry room, and I would get a few minutes at a time where I could have one boy in a bouncy saucer, another on my lap, and another playing with toys," she says. She found that the best time to work at finding vendors, creating national buzz, and building a Web site was during naptime. "I was very careful about making sure they were all on the same schedule so everyone slept

Opposite, clockwise from top left: Vendors in their booth at the show; a welcoming view of the show in its current venue, the Spokane Fairgrounds; a crowd at the show, held in a tent in earlier days; vintage merchandise is a draw.

Above: Serena, clad in an apron, doles out lunch for a Prairie Party feature in *Country Living* magazine.

Left: Lucas, then aged 7, was happy to demonstrate his crust-rolling skills when Serena did a pie-baking story for *Country Living* in 2006.

✳**HOW THE KIDS SEE IT** "We like telling jokes at the show, but at home when my mom's on the phone for work, it takes her a little bit longer to answer a question. That bugs me."

—Lucas, 10

Above: The Farm Chicks have written two books; one is a Christmas decorating book with projects and recipes, the other a cookbook with crafts.

Opposite: The entire Thompson family posing with their freshly cut tree in a shot taken for *The Farm Chicks Christmas*.

at once," she says. "And I worked late at night. I survived on very little sleep, but it was a trade-off. It was better than not spending time with the boys during the day." The one thing she made sure of was that early evenings and weekends were strictly reserved for her kids and husband. She implemented little tricks to make sure the business stayed out of her mind: turning off the computer, refusing to answer the phone after 5 p.m., and tucking away anything with a logo so she wouldn't be reminded of work.

SERENA'S BOYS HAVE ALWAYS ACCOMPANIED HER TO THE ANNUAL SHOW. When they were really young, that meant toting tubs of G.I. Joes and Lego blocks to keep them occupied. When they were a little older, she'd let them set up a stand and sell water. And when that no longer satisfied them, she found other things that did. "One year, they had a joke stand and told jokes to anyone who wanted a laugh," she says.

"I've had to get creative." For the most part, Serena says having her kids at the show has worked out okay, and she's very welcoming to other parents who bring their kids. "Women know that their kids are welcome and there are lots of moms pushing strollers or carrying babies in baby backpacks," she says.

"One year, an older woman approached me and told me she'd never come back to the show unless I stopped allowing children. I told her that children would always be welcome, and gave her a full refund on her admission. I've learned that I can't please everyone, and I just need to stay true to what I believe."

✳I THINK I CAN! "I admire the optimistic way my children look at life, and I try to keep that same attitude. In the beginning, I had no entrepreneurial experience, sources, or how-to books to draw from. So I just designed a show I'd want to be at if I were a shopper. That's all I could do."

Rebecca Rather

RATHER SWEET BAKERY AND CAFÉ

Fredericksburg, Texas
rathersweet.com

When Rebecca Rather was profiled in O, *the Oprah Magazine* a few years ago, her daughter, Frances, was impressed. It was a great moment for Rebecca, whose relationship with her daughter hasn't always been smooth sailing. A career in food service claimed so much of her time that Rebecca missed much of Frances's young life, something she says her daughter at times resented a bit. But today—after a move from Texas to New York and back again, the opening of a bakery and café of her own, the publication of several cookbooks, and a few food fights—their relationship is back on track.

✳BALANCING ACT

"When my daughter was small and wasn't in school, she'd be with me at work. She'd sit on flour sacks and keep me company. She'd draw pictures, fold napkins, sing songs with the chefs. It was a hassle for sure at times, but that's what we had to do."

THERE WAS A TIME WHEN FRANCES SPENT THE WEE HOURS OF THE MORNING ASLEEP UNDER HER MOTHER'S BREAD-MAKING TABLE. Rebecca had to report for work at 2:30 a.m., and Frances went with her. She would wake Frances up at 7, take her to school, then get back to the bread. She was recently divorced and raising Frances on her own. She had day care, and friends who would pitch in from time to time, but with bakers' hours being what they are, often Rebecca had no other option than to take Frances to work with her. "She'd stay in a playpen next to my pastry table. It was really hard to focus on work with her there, but I couldn't afford full-time help. It was not a fun time." On top of that, her male bosses weren't very understanding of her struggles as a single mom. If she had to take time off when Frances was sick, or to carpool, "they weren't very nice about it." So Rebecca left, and opened her own bakery in Austin.

After a short time, Rebecca found a space she loved in the town of Fredericksburg, sold her home in Austin, and moved, expanding the bakery into a café in its new location. That's when the trouble with Frances began. "She was such a sweet, wonderful child," Rebecca says of Frances. "So patient. But she was in eighth grade when we moved, and she did not want to move to this tiny town." Though Frances was old enough to be left alone when not in school, opening a restaurant is no easy feat, and it requires a huge time commitment. It was not the ideal situation, says Rebecca, but she didn't see any other way. To compensate, she tried to carve out family time when she could, scheduling vacations with friends who also had kids, and she fondly looks back on their visits to places like Acapulco. "I do feel like I missed out on a lot, and I was always guilt-ridden about it," she says. "I missed her track meets and golf tournaments, and she was often angry in high school about the fact that I worked so much. She gave me a hard time about it. But I don't know what I could have done differently."

REBECCA ALSO HIRED FRANCES AT THE BAKERY, HOPING TO SPEND MORE TIME WITH HER. That didn't work out so well. "She liked to use different accents while waiting on customers," recalls Rebecca. "One day she would be British, another day she'd be French. She'd make a beard and mustache with my meringue and wear it to the tables. She thought it was funny, but I was not amused. She wouldn't listen to me at all, so I actually fired her."

Now that Frances is in college, Rebecca says the two are getting along much better. It may be because Frances has outgrown her testy teenage years—or it could be because Rebecca

*✳ **OH NO THEY DIDN'T!***

Says Frances: "My mom fired me. I think it's because I have a deep-seated need to have food fights in the kitchen. There are just so many things lying around back there to fling—meringue, cookie dough, cake batter, whipped cream. I could never help myself. Sorry, Mom."

Above: Beaux, a white Pyrenees, helps mind the animals that reside at Rebecca's home.

Opposite: Hand-decorating baked goods is a painstaking and creative part of Rebecca's craft.

✳ **HOW THE KIDS SEE IT**

"My mom used to make wedding cakes, and it was horrifying for me. Making sure the gargantuan structures didn't fall to pieces in the car during delivery was bestowed upon me. Frequently, buttercream frosting plus bumpy roads equals disaster. I still have nightmares about it!"

—Frances, 23

Above: Rebecca and her daughter, Frances, smiling together with sweet success during a break when working on one of Rebecca's cookbooks, *The Pastry Queen Christmas*.

has gotten a little better at finding a balance between work and family. When Frances comes home from school in New York, she is Rebecca's main priority. "I've learned that work will always be there," she says. "You've got to take time off for family. When Frances comes home now, I try to clear my schedule and give her my undivided attention. She deserves it for putting up with my work schedule. And she likes me again—thank goodness!"

✳ **SNOWED IN TOGETHER** "When Frances was in third grade, we temporarily moved to upstate New York so I could learn to bake bread. We moved in the middle of a blizzard. We knew nobody there and spent the first night in a fleabag motel, freezing—we weren't used to the cold weather. But we both remember that time as wonderful, and have lots of great memories. We had so much fun together."

Jen O'Connor

EARTH ANGELS TOYS:
FOLK-ARTISTS' REPRESENTATIVE

Warwick, New York
earthangelstoys.com

When Jen O'Connor had her first child in 2000, she left her full-time job to stay at home with him. Discovering the baby didn't keep her busy enough, she decided to make something of her passion for folk art by promoting the work of contemporary women artists. She established an online gallery and began hosting occasional live sales events as well. It wasn't a huge leap for Jen, who had spent years as an urban planner helping local businesses in Brooklyn, N.Y.—she simply refocused her skills on artists' businesses. More importantly, when she launched Earth Angels Toys from her laptop in her kitchen, she decided it had to be the kind of business that keeps things personal. Her rule: Always mix business and pleasure.

✳BALANCING ACT

"Don't forget to mix business
and pleasure. Have the kids
help and ask your family to
attend your events. Share a
little bit of yourself with your
clients; tell them something
you've just done with your
kids. But never complain
about the juggle or the lack
of sleep—and *never* use your
kids as an excuse for why you
didn't do something."

AS THE BUSINESS AND FAMILY BOTH GREW, JEN REMAINED TRUE TO HER PHILOSOPHY. Of the business, she says: "I love beautiful, handmade things and have always been an art enthusiast and avid collector. I wanted to establish an image for the artists who create the things I love, and connect them with customers." Earth Angels Toys gave her a way to do that and it flourished. And as for family, even after her daughter was born in 2002 and another son in 2005, Jen refused to have a full-time nanny. After all, she'd left her old career and moved to the country to stay home with the children.

Having decided at the outset that she was not going to separate work and family, Jen made no effort to mask the sounds of her kids in the background when on the phone with clients, and she only hired assistants she felt close to, mixing friendship, family, and business. "I always tell my clients—old and new—when my kids are home during a phone meeting, and I'm not embarrassed by anything they may do in the background. My clients always understand. They respect the working situation I have created because most of them are moms themselves." As far as her three employees go, they are all now close friends—and she wouldn't have it any other way. "I need to have

Left: This whimsical bird toy is the work of one of the artists Jen represents.

Opposite: Jen and her husband prepare to set the stage for an Earth Angels Toys show, held several times a year on the grounds of their home.

✳HOW THE KIDS SEE IT "I help my mom by doing stuff for my brother and sister. I see that my mom's business is hard work, but I still want to have my own one day. I want to call it Great Minds Inventions."

—son, 9

Above: Jen's sales events are intentionally festive, and party hats are part of the fun, especially for the younger set.

Opposite: Artist Laurie Messeroll marks her wares with signature hangtags.

this personal comfort with employees because the business is so close to my heart," she explains. "It makes things challenging at times—working with friends and juggling their various commitments—but I would rather have these challenges than surround myself with people I cannot completely trust."

When her young kids were at home, Jen ran her business throughout the day, heading out to the Secret Lab—an outbuilding on her family's property that she had built for her work—whenever she could steal a few moments. When she needed a solid block of time to get something done, she'd hire a sitter for a few hours. And she designated late nights for herself. Even now, though the older children

✳OH NO THEY DIDN'T! "When my daughter was 22 months old, every time this one client, Robin, would call, like clockwork my daughter would come running in screaming that she needed to go 'P-O-T-T-Y!' But Robin and I ended up bonding over the silliness and have actually become great pals. Whenever she and her husband come over to visit now, my daughter loves to tell that story."

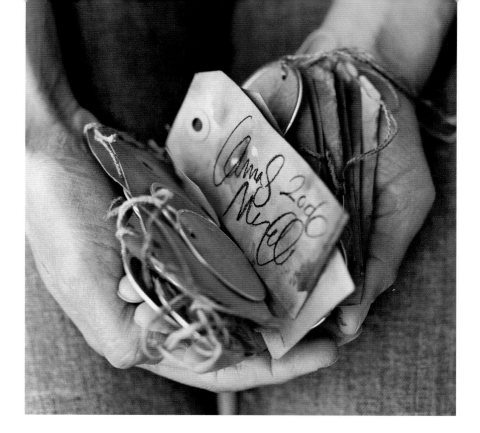

are in school, she says, "As a rule, I work late two nights a week, heading back to the computer when the kids are asleep and the house is peaceful."

FROM THE START, JEN SAYS SHE MADE IT CLEAR TO HER FAMILY THAT THIS WAS THEIR COMPANY, NOT JUST HERS. "I am always quick to remind them that this is a family business," she says. "The kids help with mailings, unpacking boxes, and whatever I can do to keep their hands busy and their hearts full." Keeping their hearts full includes making sure she takes time out to have a little fun with her kids. "It's small efforts—like making silly shapes with pancake batter, or stopping my writing to catch a firefly— that make the days sweet."

✳**MOM, UNPLUGGED** "Sometimes I choose not to turn on my computer, so I can avoid the sea of e-mails I know I have. It's a big-girl decision to understand that it can wait. I may miss a sale, but if I'm always working I could miss something in life."

Yolanda Owens

IWI FRESH: ALL-NATURAL SKIN CARE PRODUCTS

Atlanta, Georgia
iwifresh.com

When you're a single mother of three, it's hard to give up the money and security of a successful corporate career. But after making a comfortable living as a computer engineer and manager for Fortune 500 companies, Yolanda Owens outright quit one day to launch iwi fresh, a line of all-natural skin care products. The decision meant moving into a smaller home, giving up luxuries like family vacations, and convincing her extended family that she wasn't crazy. Today, Yolanda is exactly where she wants to be: whipping up products right in her own kitchen. iwi fresh has taken off, and her kids are her biggest supporters. Says Yolanda: "They tell their friends, 'My mom's going to become a millionaire!'"

"WE'RE ABOUT TO GO ON A JOYRIDE." That's what Yolanda said to her kids when she decided to quit her job and start iwi fresh. It was a risk, but it was something she just felt she had to do. She has always had a creative side. "I love working with my hands—painting, drawing, sewing," she says. She also has a grandmother with a life-long belief that drugstore products are too harsh for the skin, and that belief had rubbed off on her by the time she was at college, studying computer science and making her own natural skin care products to save money. Yolanda had no idea then that her frugal dorm-room antics would later sprout into iwi fresh. Upon graduation, she took a job in computer engineering and found herself swept into the corporate world.

As the years went by, her desire to do something more creative kept growing and in 2002, it triumphed. "I just had this burning desire to do my own thing," says Yolanda. "And then I felt this spiritual force telling me it's time to take a leap of faith." It wouldn't be easy. She was on her own and raising three kids, ages 10, 8, and 6 at the time. But she had some money saved and decided to go for it. Most of her family and friends were skeptical. "They felt that since I had a college degree and was very successful so far, I should be content," she recalls. One person

Above: Looking good enough to eat, gourmet skin care products from the iwi kitchen include face cream that gives your skin a 14-karat glow, a body oil spray made from fresh limes, and a mint face cleanser.

✳BALANCING ACT

"In the beginning, it was very challenging for me to set aside a designated 'work time.' I was working full time in my technical corporate job, being a mother, and busy starting iwi fresh. I had to learn to do small sets of tasks at a time. I set milestone dates to strive for. And I stayed positive."

✳**HOW THE KIDS SEE IT** "The only thing that annoys me about my mom's business is when I smell iwi all through the house and it gets in my nose when I'm trying to eat!"

—Jordan, 18

Above: Cutting large bricks of soap into individual bars is sometimes a family activity. Yolanda gets things set up for her kids.

was definitely in her corner, though: her elderly grandma, whom Yolanda describes as "a strong, confident, dedicated, hard-working woman who has always been my mentor."

FOR A YEAR, YOLANDA HUNG ON TO HER JOB AND STARTED IWI FRESH ON THE SIDE, working on it early in the morning and late at night. She struggled to find time for her kids, often replacing home-cooked meals with fast food. But her spirituality helped her stay focused and calm. "I kept a vision of how wonderful my business was going to be in my mind," she says. "I prayed and meditated every day to keep the exciting spirit in my heart." By the end of the year, the balancing act became too much, and Yolanda decided something had to give. She resigned from her job so she could focus on iwi fresh.

"They offered me a promotion, a pay increase, and extra vacation to stay," says Yolanda. But she stayed true to her decision and left. This freed up some time, but there were other sacrifices, including trading her spacious home for a small one, where the living room became her office, the garage was converted to a manufacturing space, and a small shed was purchased to store everything that used to be in the garage. The tradeoff was a good one: She was able to start her workday after she sent her kids off to school and focus on iwi fresh until they got home, and she was free to cook meals again. She even found time to volunteer at their school from time to time. Her mother helped care for the kids during the summers, when school was out. And Yolanda learned to multi-task so she could attend some activities with her kids. "I'd take my laptop to their swimming classes and sit by the side of the pool and work," she remembers.

THESE DAYS, YOLANDA FINDS HER LIFE MORE BALANCED, AS HER KIDS HAVE GROWN UP TO BE HER ASSISTANTS. "They're old enough now that they're able to help out," says Yolanda. "They fill containers, put on labels, and help with packing and shipping." Her biggest challenge now? Convincing her extended family that she's still busy. "My family is very supportive now and they give me encouraging words, but sometimes they add pressure by wanting me to spend more time with them. Once I left my corporate job, they felt I had all of this free time during the day!"

✳**OH NO THEY DIDN'T!**

"The funniest time I remember happened in the early stages of my business. I stored face cream in the refrigerator and my son had mistaken it for butter and ate it! But my products don't contain any chemicals, so he survived."

Above: Yolanda supervises as Janai, her stepdaughter, wields a fluted cutter while Jordan, her older son, looks on.

✳**STAYING STRONG** "I take deep breaths every chance I get to slow down. Pacing myself is key to staying healthy so I can take care of my family."

Tasia Malakasis

FROMAGERIE BELLE CHÈVRE:
ARTISAN GOAT CHEESE

Elkmont, Alabama
bellechevre.com

Most people have favorite products they purchase regularly: a certain kind of soap, a signature perfume, a brand of whole wheat bread. For Tasia Malakasis, it was goat cheese—specifically, a brand called Belle Chèvre. The online marketing executive first tried the cheese, which she noted was made by an Alabama farmer, after spotting it in a gourmet shop. She loved it. Six years later, in 2006, newly divorced, with a toddler to care for alone, she purchased the farm (really!) and took over the business. So how does one go from talking tech to herding goats? With a lot of confidence—and absolutely no regrets.

Above: The unique terrain of northern Alabama contributes a special, award-winning flavor to Belle Chèvre cheeses. They all mix wonderfully with wine, fruit, and bread.

TASIA DOESN'T BELIEVE IN ASKING FOR PERMISSION. "IF YOU WANT TO DO SOMETHING," SHE SAYS, "JUST GO FOR IT." After 15 years working in the high-tech world, she decided she wanted to try something else. She had always been intrigued by the idea of working with food, so she enrolled in a course at the Culinary Institute of America. The only problem was that she didn't want to be a chef. Then she remembered that goat cheese she fancied so much. So she had an idea: She'd buy the farm and start making the cheese herself.

Okay, it wasn't that simple. In fact, the bravery and drive it took for her to get where she is today are remarkable. Perhaps it was all those

✳BALANCING ACT

"The biggest thing, I think, is for women to be confident and okay with being working mothers. I actually see it as a good thing. When there's so much focus on children, they become selfish. Kids need to learn that moms have grown-up things to do. When you stress about trying to do so much, you feel guilty, and then you impart that to your kids."

Top: Tasia offers chèvre marinated in olive oil and spices for gift-giving, entertaining, or personal munching.

Above: All Belle Chèvre cheeses are packaged to maintain freshness and survive shipping.

Opposite: Tasia poses with a tray of fresh goat cheese logs.

years working with startup companies that led Tasia to think, "Why can't *I* learn the business of cheese making?" So she called up the farm owner in Alabama and convinced her to take her on as an apprentice, training for six months before taking over.

When Tasia realized her goal and became the head of Fromagerie Belle Chèvre, her son, Kelly, was only 3 years old. She was a single mother, and she was trading a high-tech salary for a bunch of smelly goats. "I'm sure my mom thought I was a loon, but no one's opinion mattered at the time," says Tasia. "I couldn't have any regard for fear. I felt compelled to do it, so it was more frightening for me *not* to do it. I knew that I needed to be happy or I would be a subpar mom." It was a lucrative decision. In just two years, Tasia tripled Belle Chèvre's revenue.

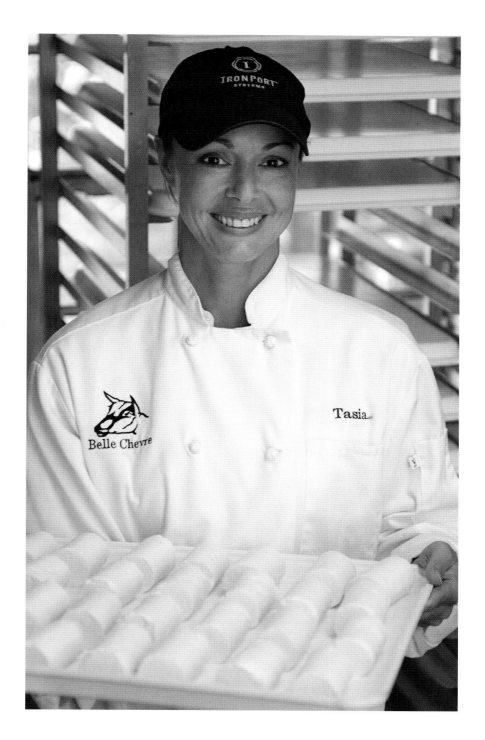

TASIA DOESN'T BELIEVE IN FEELING GUILTY ABOUT THE DEMANDS OF RUNNING A BUSINESS. Even though running Belle Chèvre requires her to spend many evenings working and to travel frequently, she simply doesn't allow herself to struggle with the work–life balance as many women do. She employs a full-time nanny who cares for Kelly when she's away. "Mothers have always had things going on, even when they stayed at home in the 1960s," she says. "Middle-class housewives had social activities. There was affordable help, and they'd be drinking martinis while their kids were off running around. The focus wasn't always on the children. There's just a different *kind* of balance now, and moms feel guilty."

Tasia does enforce one rule to make sure she and Kelly are together daily: she won't work during meal times. "Between 7 and 8 p.m., and at breakfast, that time is sacred," she says. "The phone is off and Kelly and I have family time." And when Kelly, now in grade school, needs her, he lets her know. "If Kelly isn't feeling well, and he asks for a Kelly–Mommy Day," she says. "I'll cancel all of my appointments and that's it."

"IT'S NOT ABOUT BEING WOMEN; IT'S ABOUT BEING PEOPLE, ENTREPRENEURS," she says about her philosophy of life and business. "Why do we even have *Working Mother* magazine? The term 'working father' doesn't exist because it's an assumption that he can be gone and he's doing what he's supposed to be doing. A 'working mother' is seen as an anomaly. But we shouldn't have to ask for extra permission to work."

Opposite, from top left: Tasia shares a moment of leisure with a new kid on the farm; Tasia shows Kelly how to fit packaged cheese into a shipping box; they check the quality; Kelly admires a batch of goat cheese discs.

✳ **TAKING ACTION** "I'm a zealot when it comes to being optimistic and positive. If I don't have a clean house because I haven't had the time to clean it, I have to remedy that quickly. I'll skimp on certain things so I can hire someone to clean it if I have to."

Zhena Muzyka

ZHENA'S GYPSY TEA: PREMIUM ORGANIC, FAIR-TRADE TEAS

Ojai, California
gypsytea.com

Zhena Muzyka didn't have the luxury of time to plan when she launched her business in 2000. Her infant son, Sage, had just been diagnosed with a kidney disorder. He required multiple surgeries, which meant Zhena, single with no health insurance, needed to do something to make money—and fast. In keeping with her gypsy heritage and longtime passion for tea, aromatherapy, and herbal medicine, she decided to market a product she knew well. She blended her own teas, borrowed $3,000 from friends and family to purchase a tea cart, and hit the pavement with Sage in tow. Ten years later, Sage is a healthy boy and Zhena's Gypsy Teas are sold across the United States and Canada and commended for their fair-trade cultivation.

✳BALANCING ACT

"Balance really has to come from within. We are trying to achieve health and prosperity in a hectic world. If we reach outside for balance, we may find that there isn't any. But within us, we have the tools to achieve it. For me, meditation time in the morning is crucial to my balance. I've found that the times when I'm too busy to meditate are the times when I end up feeling most overwhelmed."

WHEN ZHENA STARTED GYPSY TEAS, SAGE WAS THERE WITH HER EVERY STEP OF THE WAY, snug in a baby carrier while she wheeled her cart around. When she started selling wholesale, she brought him to meetings and tastings at Whole Foods, restaurants, cafes, and spas. She didn't have time to worry how it looked for her to be toting a baby around to meetings. She had no choice. "I needed to support my son, so the time was 'right away,'" she says. Most of the time, she remembers, "Sage was happy as a clam." But of course there were times when he'd cry and be

Above: Packaging for Zhena's Gypsy Teas is appealingly Bohemian. The teas are a blend of leaves, herbs, flowers, spices, and essential oils.

Right: Zhena in her office/showroom, before a display of the many flavors of Gypsy Tea and lots of teapots too.

fussy, and at those times, "I wasn't laughing. When you're a single mother in survival mode, every account means whether or not you're going to succeed in the long run. With Sage so unwell, there was an added level of strain and stress. It was a lot to put on a 25-year-old girl."

She did succeed. When she began, fair-trade imports were a fairly new concept, but Zhena had learned that most corporations paid tea workers very little money and didn't give them adequate health care. She didn't want to run a business that took advantage of people. While her mother watched Sage, she went to India to meet with tea growers and figured out how to operate a fair-trade business that would help end poverty for its workers. Back in California, she rented a small warehouse and started making teas in big batches from the leaves she had purchased. Then she promoted her blends as all-natural and fair-trade products. The idea caught on, and she landed one account after another. Along the way, she grew very close to her tea pickers. When she and her current husband decided to marry in Sri Lanka, it was meant to be an elopement of sorts, but her "new family" wouldn't hear of it. "My tea pickers threw us a huge, traditional Hindu wedding at a tea garden," she says. "They surprised us with three days of festivities. They really are my spiritual family."

＊OH NO THEY DIDN'T!

"Once I was driving to Los Angeles to meet with a chef, and Sage, who was with me, was hungry, so I gave him some hardboiled eggs to munch on. Well, when we got there, I was unloading the trunk—and Sage spit up all over his adorable green coveralls. There I was in the parking lot of this five-diamond resort, and my baby was a mess. Regurgitated egg and organic tea don't really go together! I went into the bathroom and frantically washed him down."

Opposite: Fair-trade practices have helped Zhena form close friendships with her tea pickers, who hosted a huge celebration when she and her husband married in Sri Lanka.

✳**HOW THE KIDS SEE IT** "I love helping my mommy come up with ideas. Sometimes she's too busy to hang out with me, but when I go to school and people ask me what my mom does, I feel so proud to tell them. I love her tea. Everybody should drink tea!"

—Sage, 10

Above: Sage, a robust 10-year-old with no remnants of the health problems that threatened his early life, shares a quiet moment with his mom, in California.

Opposite: Among the Gypsy Tea offerings are several chai blends. Each is a distinctive mix of black tea, fragrant spices, and other enticing flavors.

SAGE IS OLD ENOUGH NOW TO REALIZE THAT MOM HAS A LOT GOING ON. Zhena usually gets up at 4:30 a.m. to squeeze in a couple of hours of work before sending him off to school. She takes him out for a snack after school before returning to the office to work some more. She takes her laptop (and a big Thermos of tea) to his soccer practice, typing e-mails on the sidelines. Zhena says he pretty much lets her work without interruption when she has to at home. "I clearly communicate to him that Mommy's work is also her passion and that a mom following her bliss is a happy mom," she says. "He understands that, because he wants a happy mom. Plus, when I'm working he knows he's better off entertaining himself or I'll put him to work!"

Things have been running smoothly, but now there's a baby daughter in her life as well, and Zhena says she may have to rethink her schedule. "I'm trying to think

about how I'm going to do it all in the midst of several product launches, a growing staff, and my new baby," she says. "I'll have to start handing things over quite a bit." Perhaps she can hand some of her workload to Sage. Turns out, the young Food Network fan is a budding tea master with big ideas. "He's convinced we should launch a line of children's teas, and he's always working on formulating flavors," says Zhena. "He's insisting on a peanut butter and jelly tea. Where in the world am I supposed to find organic peanut butter flavoring for tea?"

ZHENA SAYS HER LIFE COULDN'T HAVE WORKED OUT MORE PERFECTLY. She loves that she has been able to tie together her gypsy heritage, passion for herbal remedies, and desire to have an ethical business. Raising a son, caring for a newborn daughter, and running her tea empire, Zhena is certainly busy. But juggling all this is nothing compared to what she went through when Sage was so dangerously unwell. "The idea of losing someone you love so much, as a child, is incomprehensible," she says. "Nothing else in life has been that scary for me, and I thank God daily that we made it through that."

✳**ASK FOR HELP** "I've always been independent, and I think in the beginning of my business I was a little too self-reliant. When things would go wrong, I'd just stay quiet about it. Later, when I finally started finding mentors and asking for help, my business grew tremendously. I should have asked for help sooner."

Haile McCollum

FONTAINE MAURY: PERSONALIZED GIFTS AND STATIONERY

Thomasville, Georgia
fontainemaury.com

Mothers can be our biggest inspiration in life, even after they're no longer with us. That definitely holds true for Haile McCollum, whose mom convinced her to go to art school. Once Haile received her master's degree in graphic design, it was as though someone hit the fast forward button on her life: In less than two years, she got engaged, got married, moved twice, started a business, and had her first son.

Now she's the owner and head designer for a line of personalized gifts and stationery, Fontaine Maury. The name? A tribute to her beloved mother, Fontaine.

"When the business was still run from my home, it was difficult. 'Oh, let me just check my e-mail' on a Saturday morning would turn into hours on the computer. And 'I'm just going to sweep up the kitchen quickly' became hours of household chores. Moving the business into a separate space was an important move for me."

THOMASVILLE, GEORGIA, IS A SMALL TOWN, ONE WITHOUT MANY JOBS FOR GRAPHIC DESIGNERS. When Haile and her husband moved there in 2002 after taking a year off from their careers to live in Wyoming, she wasn't sure what she was going to do. She had previously handled the stationery brand for a company in Savannah, so now she looked around her home and took inventory. "I had a computer and a desktop printer and I thought, I'll start making my own stationery and see what happens," she recalls. In April 2003 she learned that she had been accepted to the National Stationery Show in New York City. She scrambled to get ready for it. "I had the paper cutter on the kitchen table

Opposite and above: Haile's mom was mad for monograms; now Haile will add your initials or name to her stationery, tabletop items, and accessories.

Right: Work at Fontaine Maury happens here, in a building that is intentionally NOT home to the McCollum family.

✳**PITFALLS & TRIUMPHS** When Haile moved her business out of her home, she was in such a hurry to make the transition that she took newborn William on a day trip to purchase supplies. "I needed to get built-ins for the new office, so my husband and I took William on the four-hour trek to Ikea in Atlanta," she says. "He was eight weeks old—crazy! But I just figured, it had to get done."

and recruited anyone and everyone I knew to help," she says. It paid off. At the show, she picked up 80 brand new accounts. That's how Fontaine Maury came to be.

Less than a year later, her son Parker was born. At first she thought it would be fairly simple to manage everything. After all, she was working out of her home, so she'd be around to take care of Parker. A second son, William, was born a few years later, and it wasn't long before she realized the situation wasn't working. "I'm not a good home worker," she says. "I got distracted by home chores when I should have been working, and distracted by work when I should have been hanging out. I had thought that working at home would be a good thing, but I couldn't do both—work and entertain the kids—at the same time. It just wasn't fair to

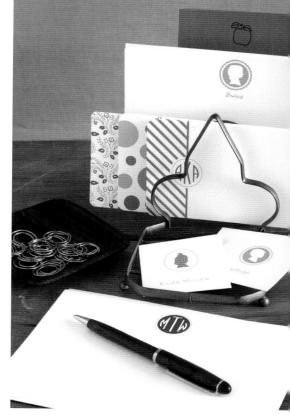

Opposite: A design board filled with colorful graphics makes a stimulating backdrop in Haile's studio, keeping interesting palettes and motifs always in view.

Left and above: The appeal of Fontaine Maury stationery and accessories designs spans generations—with a variety of graphic options available for many of the products to suit the taste of kids, teens, or adults. So yes, you may have a personalized clipboard even if dinosaurs are not your thing.

Above: William, left, and Parker keep Haile focused and disciplined about the work/family divide: She is always sure to leave her work and the studio to spend evenings and weekends with her young sons.

them." The help of a full-time nanny made things more manageable, but even so, it was hard for Haile to focus on work knowing her toddler and infant son were right in the next room.

DECIDING TO SEPARATE WORK FROM FAMILY, HAILE FOUND A SPACE AND MOVED THE BUSINESS OUT OF THE HOUSE. She's been in the new space for a few years now, and she loves it. She makes a point of leaving work at 5 every day, so she is always home for supper with the family. So far, she says, she doesn't feel she's missing anything important with her kids—though she knows that might change soon. "Of course sometimes I feel a little hurried at things like Easter egg hunts, but for the most part the kids are still so young that they don't have too many events yet," she says. "But soccer is starting soon, and I'm thinking that may be a big commitment."

Whatever comes her way, she'll handle it. After all, the company is a constant reminder of the devotion and strength of her own mother, who died of breast cancer when Haile was 23. "She was a huge part of my decision to get my master's in graphic design," says Haile. "She really made me go back to art school. So really, the whole business is a tribute to her."

✳**KEEP THINGS IN CHECK** "Having kids actually helps me stay balanced. I know I have to go home at 5, to be with them. If I didn't have that commitment, my husband and I both would probably work longer hours."

Laurie Lenfestey

BITTERSWEET DESIGNS: HANDCRAFTED JOURNALS, FRAMES, CARDS, AND JEWELRY

Santa Fe, New Mexico
bittersweetdesigns.com

Laurie Lenfestey appreciates the power of a moment. Throughout her life, she's made a point to pay attention to tiny instants—and to capture them artistically so she would have lifelong memories. "Follow your intuition, and listen to life's messages— the whispers and nudges that happen along the way." Those are the words Laurie lives by. It's that outlook on life that led Laurie to create Bittersweet Designs, a wholesale business in which she makes collage cards, frames, and journals so that others may also share, record, and celebrate life's special times.

✳BALANCING ACT

"I don't think I've sacrificed my family at all for the business. For me, it's been more about personal sacrifice—I don't have a lot of time for myself. But I wouldn't change it. I don't want to separate my family from my business, which was inspired by the cards I made for them. Life is a collage, and everything in my life overlaps. Sometimes it's hard, but that's the way I like it. It's bittersweet!"

LAURIE HEARD ONE OF LIFE'S LITTLE WHISPERS MORE THAN 10 YEARS AGO, when she and her husband moved into a new home in Santa Fe. "I noticed signs going up every Sunday across the street at the Carmelite monastery." Curious, she walked over to investigate. "Turns out, they were holding photo workshops there. I'd been wanting to learn to take better photographs, and there was one of the very best workshop facilities right across the street. It's amazing how life works—I was delighted!" She attended the workshops, and continued with her career as a real estate agent.

Above and opposite, bottom left: Laurie makes jewelry as well as paper goods. Her free-spirited pieces are made of vintage trinkets, old buttons, and semi-precious stones, which give them a Bohemian sensibility.

Opposite, top and bottom right: Vintage wallpaper and custom-designed papers that she has printed in India cover the frames, journals, and albums in Laurie's paper line; rubber stamps and ribbon and button trimmings add detail or sentiment.

When Laurie's oldest child, William, started preschool, she learned he would cry every day because he missed her. So she sent him to school with a small reminder of home. "I made him a little love letter of sorts, a collage with a photograph of us, and put it in his lunchbox," she says. "It did the trick! It made him happy, and he wanted one every day." Laurie obliged. Later she did the same for her daughter, Olivia, who is three years younger than William. It was a tradition that she continued for eight years. "It's amazing what five minutes a day can build," she says of the trinkets. "Now I have thousands of treasures celebrating our family."

In 2004, a friend suggested she make a line of cards similar to the ones she crafted for her children and attend the National Stationery Show in New York City. She did, and landed a bunch of accounts. Then she signed up for a gift show in 2005. With success there as well, she expanded her line to include journals and frames, and Bittersweet Designs was born. Laurie marvels that it all started because she read the signs—literally—across the street from her home. "Basically, I started photographing, then using those photographs for William's cards, and then using William's cards for my line of cards, and then using those cards in larger books, etc.," she says. "And so it all began!"

LAURIE WORKS IN HER "HAPPY FACTORY"—A SMALL GUESTHOUSE LOCATED BEHIND HER FAMILY'S HOME. She gets up at the crack of dawn each day so she can start working before William and Olivia are up. When the kids were small, she'd bring them to her studio and encourage them to help out, making rings, sticking stamps on things, whatever they could do. Or they'd be outside in the backyard, which she can see from her studio, playing with the dogs. "Bittersweet is all about enjoying life's special

Left and below: It was capturing life's special moments for her children, William and Olivia, that led Laurie to begin her business; now they participate, lending a hand in the studio.

Opposite: Olivia's bedroom is white and serene, decorated by her mother.

into tears at the dinner table one night proclaiming that I quit," she says. "My son promptly said, 'You can't quit, that would be stupid! At least hold on to it for a few years, otherwise it will have just been a huge waste of time.' He's my little life coach, Dr. Will."

moments, so it feels like it would be a farce if I were to exclude my kids from the business," she explains. Now that both are older, she gets them to school (she still sends Olivia off with one of her special love notes) and then spends the day working.

Laurie says not only are her kids the inspiration for Bittersweet, they're also a great support for her. William, whom she calls a "wise old soul," was the one who kept her going when she wasn't sure she could do it in the beginning. "A few months after my first show, I was so overwhelmed, and I just burst

✳**SURROUND YOURSELF WITH CALM** "I painted the floor and walls of my workspace white. I love all shades of white and cream. The studio gives me a sense of calm among the sometimes chaos of everyday life and work. I love it, and it's all mine."

Maryellen Kim

TWIST STYLE: HANDCRAFTED HOME AND FASHION ACCESSORIES

Colonial Heights, Virginia
twiststyle.com

In 2000, Maryellen Kim packed up some of her homemade creations and schlepped them—along with her children, then ages 8 and 2—to a local farmers' market. As potential buyers visited her booth, she found herself a bit surprised at their interest in her wares, and fought back the urge to shout, "Are you sure you want to pay money for this? I made it myself, in my bonus room while my kids were sticking their fingers in the paint!"

But they did want to pay money for it. In the years since, Twist Style has grown into a thriving business. Maryellen's handcrafted goods for women, children, and the home can be found online and in dozens of shops around the country—and the company has outgrown the bonus room.

"I HATED MY 'REAL' JOB," REMEMBERS MARY-ELLEN. A journalism school graduate, she was working as a writer at a daily newspaper, covering lifestyle and entertainment. "I hated the deadlines, and the pressure and politics of the newspaper business," she says. So she quit. She knew it was the right decision. "If mama ain't happy, ain't nobody happy. Plus, I decided a job wasn't worth missing all that time with my kids. I knew it would be easier to look back at missed business opportunities than it would be to look back at time I missed with my children. You get no second chances with childhood."

As soon as she felt Twist Style blossoming into a real company, Maryellen turned the bonus room over her garage into a workroom. She knew her young children would have to hang out with her while she worked, so the unfinished room was the perfect space for her at the time. "There was only sub-flooring down, which was great because the kids could draw and paint all over the floor while I worked," she explains. Once the kids outgrew their messy phase, Maryellen and her husband transformed the room, putting down hardwood floors and adding a couch and a TV so the kids would still feel comfortable there. "I was working really long days, sometimes 18 hours, and this way the family could come and keep me company and it would take the sting out of having to be so hard at work all the time," she says.

Above: Maryellen makes her Twig bracelets from semi-precious stones, with a button closure.

❊BALANCING ACT

"Balancing the kids' needs with the needs of the business is not necessarily an innate talent. You can be a wonderful mom and also a talented businesswoman, but that doesn't mean guaranteed success when you attempt to combine the two. Though the pressure can be really overwhelming at times, instead of feeling guilty, you have to remember that chances are the things that aren't getting done right now won't matter to you a month from now."

OF HER YEARS OF DAWN TO MIDNIGHT DAYS, MARYELLEN ASKS HERSELF, "WAS IT BALANCED? NO, NOT REALLY. I WORKED A *LOT!* It's not for wimps. But I feel like I had the best of both worlds, being a work-at-home mom." Maryellen says she doesn't really hit her most productive stride until late in the day, and that often results in a bit of a problem come dinnertime. "Our meal times can be really varied, as are the meals," she says. "It is not uncommon for us to have turkey sandwiches and potato chips and applesauce for supper. The meal thing is definitely my problem area. Planning and remembering to take meats out of the freezer and everything is just not my forte!"

Although at first it required some adjustment to her routine, Maryellen is happy she moved the business to a nearby office space when it got too big to operate at home. "There was no more working in my pajamas until noon, or running down to the fridge for a snack, or tossing in a load of laundry," she says. "Suddenly I had to plan—pack a lunch and be dressed and out the door early. It was a whole new world!" But now when she's home she doesn't constantly feel like she should go "upstairs" and do some more work.

Opposite, clockwise from top: The Twist Style office, painted lovely colors. A close-up view of beaded necklaces with millinery flowers. Maryellen hand-paints the fabric for these pillows, which she trims with vintage ribbon.

Above: Although she has several lines of jewelry, each of Maryellen's pieces is unique.

MARYELLEN FEELS WORKING AT HOME ALL OF THOSE YEARS WAS THE RIGHT DECISION FOR HER, as was moving the business when the children were older. "I moved at the right time," she explains, when her kids were 18 and 12. "If I had originally started this venture outside of the home, I'm not sure

✳HOW THE KIDS SEE IT "Once in a while, my mom has to go to a different state for work. But it's okay, because we make a vacation out of it."

—David, 12

things would have worked out. Even working at home, I felt bad for all those hours I put in. If I had put in all that time somewhere else—where I couldn't constantly interact with my family—it would have been really, really tough. I don't think being away from a 3-year-old all day would have made me happy. But being away now, while a 12-year-old is off at school and soccer practice and playing with friends? That's okay." Now she faces a new twist: she's expecting another baby. "This unexpected event is a GOOD thing in many ways, but one GREAT thing about it is that I am being forced to figure out how to operate the business in a much more organized and efficient way."

Opposite: The Twist Style workroom features an amazing collection of beads and trinkets.

Right: After years of hanging out in the Twist Style workroom, both of Maryellen's children are creative and enjoy lending a hand.

✳**NO REGRETS** "I've worked my booty off, but I've always put my family first. That means I've missed some big shows and fabulous opportunities for my business. But I have never felt regret like the regret I know I would feel if I had missed my daughter heading off to prom, or my son receiving a sports award."

Barbara Schriber

BARBARA SCHRIBER DESIGNS: GREETING CARDS AND WRAPPING PAPER

Sandpoint, Idaho
barbaraschriberdesigns.com

Tired of putting on stuffy clothes for work every day, Barbara Schriber decided to follow in her mother's footsteps and enter the world of crafting. But in 2007, after only four years in business, she had a baby and chose to close up shop. A year later, she found the smart financial planning she and her husband had done fell short as the economy flailed, and she resurrected Barbara Schriber Designs in order to bring in a little extra money for the family. In doing so, she learned that downsizing—and not biting off more than she could chew—is the key, for her, to being both Mom and entrepreneur.

BARBARA SAYS MOST OF HER CHILDHOOD MEMORIES INVOLVE A LITTLE BIT OF GLUE, OR STAPLES. Her mother, master crafter Melissa Neufeld, owned several retail craft stores and a paper goods manufacturing company. "When I was 11 or 12, I'd come home from school and stuff envelopes," Barbara recalls. "I couldn't sit in front of the TV without stapling or stuffing!" But even though she was surrounded by it, crafting wasn't something she ever saw for her future. "I just didn't think I had that talent, so I never tried to develop it," she says. "I worked for my mom in high school and during college, but I stuck to the business side." Her interest in business led her to a career as a financial analyst in California. But it wouldn't be long before crafting crept its way back into her life.

When her husband's job required a move to Idaho in 2003, Barbara found herself going

✳BALANCING ACT

"I think you have to allow yourself to admit that you can't do it all. And allow your house to get messy. Remember that work will always be there, but your children will grow up faster than you can imagine. And most important, have a girlfriend who understands your chaos, who will listen to you when you want to cry."

Below: A collection of vintage postcards assembled over time provides the imagery for Barbara's nostalgic, glitter-dusted greeting cards.

on interview after interview in her new hometown and coming home disgruntled. She realized she was done with corporate finance. "I came home from an interview one day and told my husband, 'I don't want to do the whole nylons and heels thing anymore.' He said, 'Then don't.' My mom was in the middle of a project and asked me to help out with the production. It turned out I had fun doing that." Borrowing a bunch of materials from her mom, Barbara started her own company, creating cards, paper goods, and gifts. Later, when she decided not to continue her business while raising her baby, James,

she says, "I couldn't do both and truly didn't want to. I wanted to be a stay-at-home mom. My husband and I had planned for having a family, so it was doable. The cost of living in Idaho is much cheaper than it is in California." But Barbara and her husband hadn't anticipated the recession and a slow-down in his business.

TO BE AS HAPPY AS A WORKING MOM AS SHE WAS BEING AT HOME FULL-TIME WITH HER SON, Barbara had to find a way to resurrect her business without taking too much time away from James. "I figured greeting cards and wrapping

paper were easy enough to do at home, so I re-launched with just those products," she says. "I got rid of 70 percent of my inventory. I sell to about 75 stores now, where I used to sell to 800. But that works for me because I don't have any overhead. It's profitable enough that I don't have to get another job, and I get to be home with James."

With a 2-year-old running around, Barbara has to be careful to keep her home workshop safe. She uses a special glass glitter imported from Germany on her designs, and in order to keep it away from James, she limits her work

Opposite: With materials in sight but absolutely tidy, Barbara's basement workroom is the dreamy home of her wholesale business.

Above: For her clients who wish to sell sweets with special appeal, Barbara provides Belgian chocolate bars in charming wrappers.

hours to his naptime; that's the only time she can sneak off to the studio in her basement. She's just had another baby, and says it may get a little tougher to work, especially if she can't get the two kids on the same napping schedule. Perhaps that would be a good time to turn again to her mom for help, this time as a sitter? Says Barbara, "Lucky for me, she's right down the road!"

✳**DO IT YOUR WAY** "I remember from my childhood that my mom wanted to be involved in every aspect of her business. But I've learned you just can't. For instance, I know I should go to the National Stationery Show in New York, but I won't. I don't want to be away from my boys for 10 days."

Amy Barickman

INDYGO JUNCTION AND THE VINTAGE WORKSHOP: FABRIC-ARTS SUPPLIES

Kansas City, Missouri
indygojunction.com and thevintageworkshop.com

When Amy Barickman started her first company, Indygo Junction, which provides materials and instructions for quilters and fabric artists, she had nothing to lose. It was 1990, and she had just received her degree in fine arts. She had no children and no real responsibilities. Twelve years later, with a 4-year-old son and another child on the way, she decided to launch a sister company that specializes in digitized vintage artwork for the same market.

This time, she did have something to lose: quality time with her kids. But she didn't let that stop her. She dove right in, turning to her longtime mentor—her mom—for help. Now running two businesses, Amy finds that the keys to her success have been keeping her worlds separate and knowing when to relax.

AMY HAS ALWAYS BEEN A FORWARD THINKER. Her sense of the excitement and growth in the quilting world prompted her to start Indygo Junction, which she turned into major supplier of goods for that market. Then, as technology for fabric artists evolved, she put her finger on the potential in meeting the needs of crafters wishing to print digital artwork onto fabric with their computers, and launched the Vintage Workshop. Amy credits her mother, a lifelong entrepreneur who sold patterns by local designers in a retail store in Des Moines, as the mentor who gave her the confidence to start Indygo Junction and invested the funds needed to launch it. When Amy felt the urge to start her second business, her mother was there for her again, as both example and helpmate. "Not only is she a fabulous saleswoman," Amy says, "but she's my personal cheerleader and provides great comfort to me when times are tough."

Above: A collage project on thevintageworkshop.com combines digitized vintage imagery and old notions.

Right: Mother-of-pearl buttons fashioned into a necklace, from Amy's Indygo Junction book *Buttonware*.

✳BALANCING ACT

"I'm convinced that if you can't draw a distinction between work time and family time, and give each its due, then you won't be able to do either one very well. When Mom is working, it means she needs to work without interruption. I explain that to my kids, and tell them that I'll have time to play later—and when I do, I'll be able to do it with my full attention."

Above: Graphic designer Erin Hill (in a top sewn from an Indygo Junction pattern) and Amy look over fabrics and embroidery in the pages of *Amy Barickman's Vintage Notions.*

Right: An embroidery featured in the August chapter of *Amy Barickman's Vintage Notions.*

Amy admits she's had a lot of help that made it possible to run the businesses while taking care of her two children. While she worked out of her home, she had a full-time sitter for the kids when they were too young to attend school. Her mom was also there for support and was able to come along to trade shows to watch the kids. Even so, there have been times when Amy felt really guilty about working so much. While time physically separated from the kids wasn't a problem for her, she felt bad about not always being there for them emotionally. "I felt emotionally pulled by my children's needs and by the needs of the business," she says. Of the challenges she faced, Amy remarks, "It was much more difficult than I ever anticipated. Having everything under one roof is great in a way, but then the

Above: Amy's book *Buttonware* explains how to make fun jewelry like this colorful brooch from buttons, ribbon, and wire.

Below: A sampling of the photos and artwork that can be purchased and downloaded at thevintageworkshop.com.

Above: Maintaining a separation between work and family doesn't mean the kids are banished from the office: An occasional visit, with time to clown around, is enjoyed by all.

AMY ALSO REALIZES THE BONUSES OF BEING HER OWN BOSS. She never has to work weekends if she doesn't want to, and she is free to take a long family vacation every summer, heading to a cottage in Michigan. "We play with cousins, kayak, hike, and pick raspberries," she says. "It refreshes my spirit, and when I head back to Kansas City I'm ready to get back in the thick of it." The vacation is something that she relishes and values immensely, and she is trying to let go of the guilt she feels about her hard work at other times. She knows that most women who work full-time are away from their kids all day, and just because her work happens to be at home doesn't mean she needs to play with her son and daughter at the same time. "When the kids were really young, I was extremely hard on myself about it," she says. "I wish I hadn't been. Looking back, I think that worrying about it so much made things much more challenging than they needed to be."

business is always there in the back of my mind, waiting to be tended to. If I was having one-on-one time with one of the kids, the worry of work was always in the background." Over time, she learned that having a separation between work time and family time is an essential ingredient to success as both entrepreneur and mom.

✳**LEAN ON SOMEONE ELSE** "Having my mother as a mentor has been a tremendous help to me. It made me realize that there are other opinions out there that are not your own but are still viable. And it also made me figure out that you don't need to go it alone. Asking for help is okay."

Jennifer Paganelli

SIS BOOM FABRICS: HOME AND APPAREL TEXTILES AND ACCESSORIES

Wilton, Connecticut
sisboom.com

After moving from New York City to the suburbs in Connecticut in 1997, Jennifer Paganelli decided to redecorate her new home herself, using vintage fabrics she found at a local flea market. Knowing her two children, Matthew, then 7, and Katie, then 4, would interrupt this endeavor, she hired a sitter for 15 hours a week. Soon she discovered the secret perk of this arrangement: The sitter could sew! Jennifer was thrilled

when her home was filled with items of her design, crafted with the sitter's assistance. When her husband suggested that others might like her designs too, she decided to find out whether he was right. Today she designs fabric for a wholesale firm and sells a variety of home goods, fashions, and accessories.

✳**BALANCING ACT** "The downside for me has been the lack of routine. It's hard to carve out a routine and just as you get into your groove, the bus comes and your kids are home. Also, the day-to-day interruptions are hard. I'd feel crazy when someone missed the bus, or forgot their gym shorts, homework, or lunch money. But I just tried to get a project done in stages."

JENNIFER HAS NO PROBLEM ASKING FOR HELP. In a sense, it's that willingness to lean on others that led to the creation of her company, Sis Boom Fabrics. After all, it was the desire to free up time for herself that gave her the serendipitous sewing assistance she later translated into a flourishing business. She recalls that when she decided to hire the sitter shortly after her family relocated, "Someone mentioned that my neighbor had five kids and no help, referring to that as sainthood. But I just knew that for me that wasn't going to work. I needed help, and I wasn't worried about what others thought. I needed time for me—to create—in order to be happy and balanced."

Jennifer used some of her free time to frequent flea markets, bringing home cool vintage fabrics she loved. Then she discovered the skills of her sitter. "At first it was repairs, and then she would run out to the barn with the fabrics I would buy on Sundays and work on my sewing machine. Eventually, she was sewing every time she came over and I was watching my own kids!"

JENNIFER SAYS SHE COULDN'T IMAGINE RUNNING THE COMPANY IF SHE DIDN'T HAVE PART-TIME HELP WITH THE KIDS. She produces everything for Sis Boom in a 500-square-foot studio in her home. Her home goods, fashions, and accessories are sold on her Web site and she also holds two shows a year in her house; her fabrics are distributed by their manufacturer. "When your days are defined by the kids, no matter what agenda or plan you have, things always change," she says. "When the kids were small, I would wait for the 'perfect moment' to create. But any creative person knows that can't be set up.

Opposite, top left and right: A childhood in the U.S. Virgin Islands exposed Jennifer to a world of colorful textiles; they influence her own fabric designs. The paper dolls wear skirts made of photocopies of Sis Boom fabrics.

Opposite, bottom left and right: Jennifer styles her porch for a Sis Boom show. Her advice for combining fabrics? "Go crazy!"

Above: Katie and Matthew, here captured young with their mom, have gone with the flow as Sis Boom flourished at their home.

Jennifer says both Matthew and Katie have helped out with the shows since they were very young. (Katie makes and sells dog treats to raise money for research into Lyme disease, which she had in fifth grade.) And while every room of the house is staged when it's time for a Sis Boom show, Jennifer says the kids never minded. In fact, she says, they were often sad when a show was over and things went back to normal. "I remember saying to my son once, 'I promise when the show is finished I'll get those pillows out of your room.' And he responded with, 'But then my room won't be beautiful!'" These days, Matt shares the experience with his girlfriend, who Jennifer says is a fan of the girls' clothes she makes. And if he's reluctant to help out, Jennifer knows how to persuade him: "Teenagers are the best. Sometimes disgruntled, yes, but if money is mentioned they hop to!"

I wanted to be the mother who floated around her kids, in and out of their space but very attentive to their needs, but it didn't work for me. I needed to employ some help."

✳ **TO EACH HER OWN** "Every mom has to come to terms with what keeps her sane and happy. For me, that was time for myself. I find that with work and employing some help during the week, I'm a better mom."

Mia Galison

EEBOO CORP.: GAMES, ACTIVITIES, AND GIFTS FOR KIDS

New York, New York
eeboo.com

Many women fantasize about working at home when they have kids, figuring it will allow them to spend more time with their family. That's one of the reasons Mia Galison decided to start eeBoo, a line of creative and educational children's toys, games, and activities: While already raising a toddler, she learned she  was pregnant with twins. However, she quickly discovered that eeBoo was more demanding than she had calculated, and she didn't have a whole lot of time to spend with her kids after all. But she's implemented a few quality plans that go a long way to ensuring good family bonds and business success. And in the end, she knows it will all be worth it.

✳BALANCING ACT

"When I started eeBoo, I thought my kids would always know that I was doing this for them, and for us as a family. I thought, if I weren't doing this, I'd have to be working for someone else, who might not let me leave to take them to the dentist. Unfortunately, they weren't always forgiving about the time I spent working. If you have to work—for yourself or for someone else—you're going to miss important times."

FORESEEING A NEAR FUTURE FILLED WITH KIDS' SCHOOL EVENTS AND PLAY DATES, MIA KNEW SHE HAD TO CHANGE HER WORK SITUATION. "As soon as I learned I was having twins, it was clear that it would be impossible to work for anyone else ever again," she says. That was in 1994; she and her husband had a 1-year-old son, Eyck, and at the time, she was developing the gift division for a New York City publishing house. She had already learned what she needed to start her own business. She had plenty of ideas and contacts, and she had a passion: children's toys.

What she didn't have was an abundant cash flow. So she and her husband, Sax, made sacrifices. They converted a large bathroom in their New York City apartment into a small bedroom for Eyck, and Mia used his original room as her workspace until the twins were born, when they took it over. Then she and Sax, a children's book

Above and right: Mia shows off a selection of eeBoo graphics and games. When toddlers, her children were the ideal models for eeBoo wearables.

Opposite: Finn and Eyk stop by Mia's office after school to help with a promotional mailing.

❋HOW THE KIDS SEE IT "One of the jobs I enjoy most is packing up boxes with samples to send out. I love choosing different colored wrapping paper and positioning each product to look as colorful as possible. Sending out chocolate at Christmas is the best—especially when I get to eat the few pieces I've slipped into my pocket when my mom isn't looking."

—Elodie, 13

Above, from left: Mia started eeBoo in a bedroom in her Manhattan apartment. Exhibiting at the New York International Gift Fair is an important part of eeBoo business; a colleague helps her man her booth.

illustrator, rented a basement apartment in their building as a studio to share, subletting two of the rooms to help with the rent. "There were literally places where the ceilings were only five feet off the floor, because of pipes," she remembers, "and my husband is six-foot-two!"

eeBoo took off—and with success came work. A lot of work. Mia soon realized that she didn't get to see her kids much after all. Her mother, her husband, and a part-time sitter took turns caring for the three toddlers while Mia spent all day in the basement studio. She'd get upstairs just in time to feed the children—she made a point never to miss a meal with them—and put them to bed, and then she'd head right back to the basement until 1 or 2 in the morning. It's a time she looks back on with a bit of regret. "I feel like I missed a tremendous amount of my children's early life, and I hate that," she says. "I wish I had spent more time with them during the weekdays—taken them to the park, or to the bookstore, or the grocery store. It's easy to say that now, but at the time I felt like I couldn't move from my desk."

TO SCHEDULE QUALITY TIME WITH HER FAMILY, MIA SET UP CERTAIN RITUALS DURING PARTS OF THE DAY WHEN SHE WASN'T WORKING. Every morning, before she starts her workday, she and her husband walk the kids to school. Then she and Sax take a two-mile stroll around Central Park, just the two of them. Every Tuesday night, they take one child out to a special dinner, rotating among the three so each gets his own special night. "When one of them is alone with us, we really get to communicate with each other better," she explains. They've been doing this

Below: The renovated ballroom that is now the home of eeBoo headquarters is a sure sign of Mia's success—and much airier than its bedroom and basement predecessors.

✳**PITFALLS & TRIUMPHS**
"One holiday the kids and my mother were helping me with a large order. They were sprawled out in the basement tying peppermint sticks together with ribbon. It was mayhem—there were boxes of candy sticks in every color spread out in every direction, and it was impossible to walk anywhere. No one moved when a delivery guy showed up with palettes piled with catalogs. There was no place to put them and he could not understand what he was seeing."

Above: Mia and her husband, Sax, with their three kids who, since toddler age, have helped pack, model, and inspire eeBoo wares.

since Eyck was 4; he's now 15, and the twins, Elodie and Finn, are 13.

Mia and her husband are no longer working out of a five-foot-high basement. Far from it—they now operate out of a huge renovated ballroom they rent near their apartment. It's spectacular, but Mia sometimes finds herself longing for the old days when her tiny tots would pester her in the basement. "It's funny," she says, "they used to come into the studio and I'd tell them to go away—I still feel bad about that. Now that my office isn't in my apartment building, my kids don't stop by every day. And I miss that." The upside is no more journeying back to the studio after dinner. Once Mia is home, she's home.

✳**NO RISK, NO GAIN** "I was very afraid to put the financial security of my family on the line. On the other hand, I knew I was extremely vulnerable working for someone else. If I did it myself, then at least I had some control and no one could fire me."

Libby Wienke

HAPPY MONKEY: KIDS' ACCESSORIES AND TOYS

St. Louis, Missouri
www.happymonkeydesign.com

When Libby Wienke had her first child in 2000, she quit her job as an advertising account executive so she could be with him full time, but it wasn't long before nonstop *SpongeBob* and Cheez-Its started to wear on her. So in 2002, after giving birth to her daughter, she made the decision to go back to work—this time for herself. After two unsuccessful attempts at starting a company, the arrival of a mail order catalog one day inspired her to launch Happy Monkey, a kids' product design company. Now Libby spends her days in the studio above her garage designing wall art, bedding, rugs, lighting, and other accessories—and watching the Cartoon Network.

✳**BALANCING ACT** "There's no right answer to the having-it-all question. Some days, things go right and other days they don't. I accept that. In the long term, I just hope I'm showing my kids that with motherhood and career, one doesn't preclude the other. It's also good for them to see Dad being 'the housewife' when I'm in Chicago!"

HAPPY MONKEY WAS BORN NOT FROM A DESIRE TO MAKE MONEY BUT A NEED TO ESCAPE.
"I love my children dearly," says Libby, "but many days I was counting the minutes to naptime so I could have some thoughts that didn't include potty training, drool, and shrieks of 'Swiper, no swiping!' [a line from *Dora the Explorer*]. I saw having a business as a treat, something special I would get to do for myself."

The catalog Libby found in her mailbox that day in 2002 was from the Land of Nod, the children's branch of Crate & Barrel. She was so impressed with their aesthetic that she decided to design her own kids' products, like bedding, rugs, toys, and wall art. Her husband, a graphic designer, already had the necessary computer software to create a portfolio, so she taught herself how to use it and got to work. When she

Opposite: Libby in her above-garage office, a few years after launching Happy Monkey.

Below: Happy Monkey's large, fabric-covered letter cutouts can be used as wall art to spell names or words. Libby arranges fabric swatches in flower collages as part of her design process.

finished, she mailed it out to the very company that had inspired her. As luck would have it, the Land of Nod was looking for a contract designer at the time, and the next thing she knew, Libby was driving from St. Louis to Chicago for a meeting with the head of the company. Having landed them as a client, Libby now finds herself running a successful business, flying to Chicago about six times a year—something that she both appreciates and dreads. "I look forward to the trips, to dressing in something other than a T-shirt and jeans," says Libby. "But I hate to fly. Many times I've furiously scribbled my last will and testament on the inside of a book cover."

ONE HUGE MOTIVATOR FOR LIBBY IN STARTING HER BUSINESS WAS HER MOM. "She didn't finish college, yet she worked her way up from a sales clerk to the upper levels of mass retail, as a department store buyer and area manager, and later launched her own gift shops," remembers Libby. "I've always wanted to measure up to that in her eyes and my own." Mission accomplished, Libby now notices a major difference between her own childhood and that of her kids. "When I was young, my mom had to work full-time outside of the home to support two children, and I craved seeing her. On the other hand, I'm always home. So instead of craving my time, my kids take me for granted.

They treat me like a comfortable old shoe. Whichever way you go, you can't totally win." Libby says she has learned to accept that she is never going to be perfect in every area of her life, and that's how she gets through the tough times. "Sometimes I don't tuck the kids in at night because I have a deadline. Other times, I miss an important business call because I'm driving 15 friends home from the pool. No matter what choices I make, I'm going to screw something up! I've made peace with that."

To an outsider, Libby's situation looks idyllic. From the studio above her garage, she looks out at her backyard and watches her kids—Tucker is now 10 and Kate is 7—having water balloon fights and playing kickball. In her own words, it's a bit like a Norman Rockwell painting. But the grass is not always so green. "It's a blessing and a curse," says Libby. "There are constant interruptions, like 'Mom! Tucker won't let me be Anakin!' or 'Kate hit me first!' There are many, many times when it feels less like a business and more like barely controlled chaos."

✳ OH NO THEY DIDN'T!

"One afternoon, I was on a business call with Nod when my son flew into the studio from the backyard and raced to the bathroom. He didn't close the door and started to urinate—really loudly. I swear it was like standing next to a horse! I tried to speak louder to cover the noise, just hoping they didn't think it was *me*. It's moments like that when I wish I could fire my kids!"

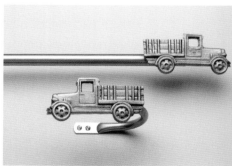

Opposite: Libby contemplates color palettes for her line.

Above: Pickup trucks are among the finial choices Libby has designed for kids' curtain hardware (chocolate-mold bunnies are another option).

Left: These print-covered boxes provide pretty storage for dress-up costumes, doll clothes, trinkets, small toys, and other little girl essentials.

✳**HOW THE KIDS SEE IT** "I like having my mom work from home because she doesn't have to drive and waste fuel."

—Tucker, 10

LIBBY FEELS THE PAYOFF OF RUNNING HER BUSINESS FROM HOME IS GREAT— DESPITE THE OCCASIONAL MAYHEM. Not only does she enjoy the freedom to take off when she wants to pick her kids up from school or volunteer on a field trip, but she has product guinea pigs at her disposal. "My kids have modeled everything from backpacks to fairy costumes so I can check construction and fit. And some of Kate's drawings have ended up on a bedding set. Some of my favorite things never made it to the sales floor, but I get to see them every day in my kids' rooms."

Above: Libby and Kate look over the letter cutouts while Tucker relaxes on one of the comfy chairs that make the studio welcoming.

✳**TIMING IS EVERYTHING** "I have some ideas of where I want to go next, but I'm not ready to upset the good balance I have just yet. Maybe when my kids are older and I'm not cool enough to hang around with."

Vicki Mote Bodwell

WARM BISCUIT BEDDING: CHILDREN'S ACCESSORIES AND TOYS

New York, New York
warmbiscuit.com

After running Warm Biscuit Bedding, her nursery furnishings company, out of her bedroom for three years, Vicki Mote Bodwell decided things were getting a little too close for comfort. The final straw that sent her looking for commercial space was a postage stamp fiasco involving her then 3-year-old son, Fischer. Ironically, once she physically separated herself from her kids during the day, she found she was able to spend more time with them in the evening. Today, with the office removed from their apartment, and with many planned family days, a no-work rule when Vicki is home, and her husband on staff, the family enjoys a closeness that's perfectly warm and comfortable.

✳ BALANCING ACT

"Working for yourself is a completely different animal from working for someone else. The number one thing is that there is no clear delineation between professional and personal. It all melds together. I would be answering phones, doing accounting, sending out catalogs, organizing photo shoots, and all the while breastfeeding or pumping in between. It was a lot of fun, but I did feel out of control for most of it."

EXPOSURE TO AN EMPTY NICHE IN THE WORLD OF NURSERY FURNISHINGS PROMPTED VICKI TO BEGIN WARM BISCUIT. In the mid-90s she was working in magazine publishing, and she would frequently hear pregnant women complaining about the lack of affordable stylish bedding and accessories for babies. "I thought, 'Hmm . . . I love fabric, decorating, and children.' Sounded like a fit!" Without leaving her magazine job, she went to work for herself, creating a catalog and Web site to sell textiles and eventually furniture and toys designed by artists she enlisted. While developing the concept, she found out she was pregnant, and by the time she took her first order, in May 1998, her son Fischer had been born. She continued to work in her bedroom, with her son often napping right there amid the photo shoots,

Above: Warm Biscuit Bedding Co. invites you to take your pick of patterned and pictorial drawer pulls—they feature decoupaged motifs applied to handpainted bases.

design sessions, and envelope-stuffing. When she was two years into the business, her second son, Henry, was born and she decided not to return to her full-time job.

By the time Vicki made Warm Biscuit her only professional commitment, she had a staff of three working alongside her in her bedroom. She'd get the kids ready for the day, then quickly scramble to tidy up before her employees arrived. She felt good about being home with her sons, but also somewhat guilty about not being emotionally available every minute. "I'd sometimes just pop in a video, or have them watch TV," she says. "I remember thinking, 'This is not what I want to do,' but I had to work." She hired a sitter, but it was nearly impossible to keep the boys out of the room—or to keep herself away from them. "It was hard for my toddlers when they knew Mom was just in the next room. They would

❋ PITFALLS & TRIUMPHS

"Fischer and his friends would always be popping the bubble wrap, or hiding inside boxes and building forts out of them. I remember many an occasion when he would be so upset because I had to throw out the boxes!"

Below: To make decorating easy for Warm Biscuit customers, Vicki creates themed ensembles of kids' bedroom furnishings; included are bedding and all sorts of small furniture, accessories, and toys. Shown here are the Pirate, Capeside Cottage Floral, and Vintage Fire Truck designs.

Above: Warm Biscuit fabrics include many classic and vintage prints. Soft furnishings can be made to order or you can purchase fabric by the yard.

changer for our family," she says. "It gave me more of a clear dividing line. It was very freeing. And it was good for the kids too. They were able to have their whole home back and have play dates without all the work noise. And I could still go home for lunch and see them."

IT TOOK SEVERAL YEARS FOR VICKI TO LEARN HOW NOT TO DEVOTE TOO MUCH TIME TO WORK—even after separating office and home. She says that while moving out was good for the business and the family, there was still a lot of takeout food, years without vacations, and envy of women (and men, like her husband) who worked for someone else and could let go of the job when they got home. "It's hard to ever step out of your own business at the end of the day," she says. "I work six days a week, and for the first eight years I rarely took any time off. I would get jealous if someone I knew went on a family vacation for a month. And I felt like my husband could just go off to work, and stay at hotels when he was traveling for business, and I still had to do it all!" But, she says, her husband has always been wonderful with helping her out when she was feeling overwhelmed. "One birthday, he sent me to a hotel for the weekend in the city," she

come in and out several times throughout the day. It was also easy for me to get sidetracked and run into the other room to handle problems or see what the chaos was all about."

"THERE CAME A POINT WHERE I STARTED TO GET ANNOYED VERSUS CHARMED" BY THE INTERACTION OF BUSINESS AND BOYS, Vicki recalls. In the fall of 2001, "Fischer found some 'stickers'—postage stamps—and stuck them all over a piece of paper," she recalls. "I lost it! I was unreasonably mad that the stamps were ruined, and that was it. I was just fed up with the casualness of the bedroom office environment." She found herself an office space and moved Warm Biscuit into it. That, she says, was the best decision she ever made. "It was a game-

✳**HOW THE KIDS SEE IT** "Sometimes my mom comes home late because something happened at work, but usually it's okay because I like going there and helping out. Sam is an art person there, and she asks me to get stuff for people, which is fun. I'm never bored because I can play with everything there. But I want a dog. I'm begging my parents for one."

—Fischer, 11

says. "I read a good book, ordered room service. It was perfect."

Vicki's husband signed on full time at Warm Biscuit after losing his job as a consultant in the energy business. She says they both still work a lot, but they're getting much better at designating family time. Every Sunday, they work from 3 p.m. to 8 p.m. and then go off to dinner alone. They have weekly family dinners, and once a month, the entire family (including their third son, Wesley) goes out and does something fun. "It might be a museum, a movie, a concert, or some sort of adventure," she says. "A little treat to keep us all bonded." As for family vacations? Vicki finally took the plunge this past year and did what she'd spent the previous 10 years watching other families do.

Above: The Bodwell family takes vacations seriously—if not as often as they'd like—leaving all thoughts of business far behind.

"I spent six weeks in Australia with everyone!" she says. "I'm getting better at carving out family time. I definitely don't get to join the PTA, though!"

✳**REINTERPRETING "BUSY"** "We were both already busy. So this was just a new busy—and it was fun, mysterious, and satisfying."

Carrie Raphael

RAPHAEL DESIGNS: INTERIOR DESIGN
AND HOME ACCESSORIES

Port Republic, Maryland
raphaeldesigns.com

Now ages 9 and 10, Emma and Noah Raphael paint Easter eggs on Halloween, sit in at board meetings, and live in a house where the walls are repainted weekly. To them, this is totally normal. Their mother, Carrie, an interior designer, stylist, and custom accessories maker, often hosts magazine shoots right in their home, and she's included her kids in her business from day one. In the time since diapers and preschool, with the help of her husband and brother, Carrie has turned Raphael Designs into a successful company—and a true family affair.

"I LEARNED THE ART OF SETTING UP A HOUSE AND MAKING EVEN THE BLANDEST OF SPACES FEEL LIKE HOME WHEN I WAS VERY YOUNG," says Carrie, who grew up an army brat, moving with her family every couple of years. It was a lifestyle that taught her to settle into her surroundings fast. But when she had her own kids, she was determined to stay in one place. "I wanted my children to grow up in a home that they would never move from, that was warm and settled."

In 2001, when Emma was 2 and Noah 1, Carrie and her husband, Charlie, moved into an old farmhouse. It was in need of work, but Carrie was up to the challenge. After all, when newly wed, she had decorated their first apartment with barely "two pennies to rub together. I wrapped weighted cardboard boxes with sheets to use as tables, painted hand-me-down furniture, and made artwork out of specialty papers, sort of like origami," she remembers. She dove into the farmhouse renovation, frequenting antiques fairs and creating a distinctive ambience in the house. When it was finished, a friend asked whether she could take photographs to send to a magazine. Carrie was surprised—she never considered herself a professional—but agreed. Within a month, a camera crew was at her new home to shoot a magazine spread.

Right: Whether planning a design project or marketing her business, collaboration is key for Carrie and her business-partner husband, Charlie.

✳**BALANCING ACT**

"Recently, as I was cooking dinner, the usual board members—the family, including my brother—were discussing the possibility of a new name for the company, and the kids were consumed with coming up with one. Emma actually sketched a logo for her concept. That night, they both kept yelling out ideas from their rooms. Their heads were just spinning with creativity! They might not understand it yet, but their help is ever-present in my life."

✳**OH NO THEY DIDN'T!** "When Emma was 3, her preschool teacher called the children outside to play by the color of their shirts. When she yelled out 'Blue!' Emma didn't move. Thinking my daughter didn't know her colors, she asked Emma why she hadn't gotten in line. Emma looked at her very seriously and said, 'My shirt is periwinkle, and you haven't called that yet.' I was so proud!"

Opposite: Carrie thinks of furniture as dress forms and its covering as clothing.

Top: A lovely studio with lots of light, a huge design wall, and curtained storage closets is home to Carrie's creative process.

Left and Above: Small sachets made by Carrie from vintage fabrics are handy as props for her shoots and make great gifts too.

Above: Sewing supplies and small props are always at hand behind the curtained doors of the closets that line one wall in Carrie's studio.

husband to handle the marketing, and her brother, Andrew, to help out with painting, networking, administrative duties, and whatever else needs doing. Her kids were right there in the middle of the excitement and growth, but never having known a different life, it all made sense to them. "There have been times when the front foyer of the house was painted three different colors in the span of a week because of shoots," Carrie says. "The kids didn't even blink."

IT WAS JUST NATURAL TO INCLUDE HER KIDS IN EVERYTHING SHE DID, Carrie felt, rather than separate her work from her family. "For me, there is a fine line between work and family life," she says. "And it's been a positive experience for us because we're together most of the time." She schedules her projects around her kids' school and social events, and Noah and Emma help her out with work, setting tables and styling props for shoots. Carrie laughs as she recalls the October in which she did an Easter story for a spring magazine issue. "It was Halloween, and we were carving pumpkins and painting eggs at the same time, " she says. "All around the house were Easter baskets and spring flowers. Noah and Emma thought it was very funny that it was

One thing led to another, and before Carrie knew it, she was styling shoots and working with private clients. Today she sells handmade products on her Web site as well. It wasn't a planned venture, but it was certainly a blessing—Charlie lost his marketing job when his firm downsized, and they needed Raphael Designs to support the family. Carrie quickly enlisted her

Easter in our home as they were leaving to go trick-or-treating."

When she has to travel to a project site, Carrie often includes her kids, bringing them along if it's a road trip. She considers these ventures both learning opportunities and bonding experiences. When Noah was 4, she took him to Washington, D.C. As they were driving along Diplomat Row, she pointed out the architecture, explaining what the different columns and moldings were. Later, Noah drew her a picture: an exact replica of a building they had seen, complete with every single architectural feature labeled. Emma's

Above: All four Raphaels share a passion for Carrie's design business, so drawing a line between work and play is rarely an issue.

domain is antiques hunting. "It's just girl time, a few times a year," Carrie says of the mother–daughter road trips. "When we're driving, we have wonderful conversations, without any interruptions."

CARRIE SAYS THERE'S ONLY ONE THING ABOUT HER INTERIOR DESIGN BUSINESS THAT BUGS HER KIDS: "The major problem I think they have is the 24-hour period before a photo shoot when the house is not their home—it needs to stay *very* clean."

✳**A FAMILY BUSINESS** "My business has been formed in a very organic way. I can't say I woke up one day and said, 'I'm starting a business. I will do A, B, and C.' I just keep waking up every day and doing what I love. I've been able to do that because I've been blessed by a family that lives this *with* me."

Monique Keegan

ENJOY CO.: HOME AND LANDSCAPE DESIGN, CONSTRUCTION, AND ACCESSORIES

Granville, Ohio
enjoyco.net

Monique Keegan, interior and landscape designer, home accessories shop owner, and mother of one, believes in seeing the big picture. She doesn't "do things piecemeal." Professionally, she provides complex services to her clients—coordinating renovation, construction, and landscaping as well as interiors—and makes sure she has a complete vision of a project before moving forward at all. Such a business philosophy requires a lot of planning and thought. It's the same way she runs her family: With meticulous scheduling, she keeps everything on track.

MONIQUE AND HER HUSBAND HAD TAKEN GREAT PLEASURE IN RENOVATING THEIR OWN PROPERTIES, AND PEOPLE TOOK NOTICE. Over the years, they'd moved several times, and three of their homes were featured editorially and on local tours. When Monique's husband, a design consultant who had worked at home, took a full-time job in 2004, she left the fashion retail world and her job as design director for Lane Bryant to pursue her passion for home renovation and spend more time with her son, Maxfield. With her unique design aesthetic—a blend of vintage, industrial, natural, and contemporary she calls "timeless modern"—success came quickly to Enjoy Co.

✳BALANCING ACT "As I'm in business longer, it does seem that I am working more than I am playing with the family. I love what I do! My work is my hobby, so it's hard to stop. I'm constantly looking at home inspiration whenever I get a free minute. I find, however, that if I make it a priority, family time can fit in. But I definitely need to schedule."

Above: A brick wall adorned with old signage from the New York City subway system demonstrates Monique's philosophy of creating a simple palette of textures and forms that reflect a homeowner's persona.

At first she did everything—sketching, research, accounting, and storage of swatches, samples, and products—in a 14' by 14' room in the home she shared with her husband and son. It was, to say the least, a tight fit. "My family couldn't even fit in there if they tried!" she says. "It was packed, and I was constantly expanding out to the island in the kitchen. It wasn't good." She moved to the basement, and then out to the barn. Also crammed into the barn along with her design materials? Maxfield. In second grade at the time, he'd hang out in the studio with his mom after school. "He had a desk in there where he would sketch cars and stuff while I worked on projects," she says. "We 'worked' side by side."

Opposite, clockwise from top: The exterior of Monique's studio and store—an old gas station she renovated. Impeccable landscaping replaces the pumps. Monique and her son, Maxfield, out shopping. A vintage advertising sign adds whimsy to an otherwise contemporary look.

Top: A blend of old and new furnishings with a few industrial accents gives this living room Monique's signature "Timeless Modern" look.

Above: A tabletop display in the retail shop portion of the Enjoy Co. premises.

project, but over time I realized that I was more efficient if I set work times and did household duties separately." Now she has a calendar on which she literally pencils in blocks of time. She starts with family stuff and then fills in work around that. "My son is my priority, as he's the reason I left my full-time job. I fill my calendar with Maxfield's and my husband's commitments first. Then I work around those appointments."

Monique says for the most part, she has been able to be there for

Left: Monique calls on her stylist's eye to arrange merchandise in her shop.

Below: Huge glass doors fronting the old garage bays shed copious light on the assorted wares that typify Monique's design sensibilities.

But since Monique makes a point of having all materials on hand before beginning a job, even the barn wasn't large enough for her business. In 2009 she purchased a former auto body shop, converted it to a studio and a retail space, and moved Enjoy Co. into it.

"I DISCIPLINED MYSELF TO ESTABLISH CONCRETE BLOCKS OF TIME FOR WORK AND FOR FAMILY," Monique says of her ability to balance the two. "At first I was doing laundry while researching a

✳**HOW THE KIDS SEE IT** "I like helping out my mom with stuff like mowing and cleaning the store. But I don't like it when customers stay in the store past closing and make Mom work late!"

—Maxfield, 11

Maxfield after school because she plans work appointments for the morning, right after dropping him off. She also hired an assistant who has a young son herself. This way, when Monique has client visits, her assistant can bring her son along and watch both boys. Since she's opened a retail store, though, time management has gotten a little stickier. "I've missed a few soccer games and things," she says. "The next goal is to figure out how to plan meals in advance too, so they don't fall by the wayside."

Right: Family time is a priority—and a pleasure— that Monique schedules along with her business obligations so she is sure to enjoy it.

✳**RULES ARE MEANT TO BE BROKEN** "My son is so flexible about my schedule and easygoing about me having to sometimes work late. So I, in turn, try to be open to doing things out of the ordinary. I'll close the shop if it's slow, and I'll shift work things around if we have the opportunity to do something spontaneously fun."

Monique Greenwood

AKWAABA BED & BREAKFAST

Brooklyn, New York
akwaaba.com

When you run your own business, it can be tough not to bring work home with you. So imagine what happens when your business *is* your home. Monique Greenwood turned an aged Italianate mansion in Brooklyn into a bed and breakfast—naming it Akwaaba, which means "welcome" in the language of Ghana—and moved in with her family. In the beginning, privacy was limited, and her young daughter encountered a never-ending rotation of guests. But Monique made it work, and discovered some unexpected perks along the way.

BACK IN 1995, WHEN SHE SPOTTED HER DREAM HOUSE, MONIQUE KNEW HER LIFE WAS ABOUT TO CHANGE. At the time, she was comfortable with her life, happily married with a 3-year-old daughter, Glynn, and enjoying a successful career as a magazine editor in New York City. The house was an old, dilapidated mansion in Brooklyn, but "I just fell in love with it and had to find a way to make it make sense," she recalls. In order to afford the mortgage and renovation, there was only one thing to do: Turn it into a bed and breakfast, and use the revenue from guests to help foot the bill.

And that's exactly what she did. The family moved into the top floor as renovations began on the rest of the house. Nine months later, they opened their doors to guests. That's when the hard work really began. Monique's days went something like this: Wake up and get ready for her magazine job. Cook breakfast and serve guests at 8 a.m. Take Glynn to preschool. Go to the office. After a long day, come home to the inn, return phone messages and call back to schedule reservations, clean the empty guest rooms, go to bed, get up, and do it all over again. While she had help from her husband, who took care of Glynn after work, her brutal schedule began to weigh on her. "I started getting jealous of my guests," she says. "I'd come home from

Above: When she opened her fourth inn, in New Orleans, Monique, her husband, Glenn, and their daughter, Glynn, welcomed friends and former colleagues from Monique's publishing career to the opening party: "A blast!"

✳**BALANCING ACT**

"When you talk about balance, it's related to scales. So if you put work on one side and family on the other, remember that there's a stem in the middle. And that stem is you. *You* can't be off balance or the scale won't work. So every day, I ask myself, 'Where do I fit in?' Even if it's just taking a morning walk every day, you have to do something to stay balanced."

work and see them sitting by my fireplace, sipping my tea, and I'd have to stand outside and fix my attitude before I could walk inside." So about six years into it, she made the decision to quit her day job to focus on the inn full time.

LIVING IN AN INN IS AN ODD THING BECAUSE YOU'RE PRETTY MUCH SHARING YOUR HOME WITH STRANGERS. There are definite sacrifices to be made in order to respect boundaries. For example, Monique had to start labeling everything in the kitchen—food for guests, and food for family. And the whole family had to be conscious of their visitors at all times. "We can't cook fish or the whole house will smell!" she points out. It's her husband, she says, who

✳**PITFALLS & TRIUMPHS** "In the early days of running the inn, on Sundays, when my daughter and I would go to the movies, I'd fall asleep in the theater every time. She actually had to tell me to stop snoring! She'd be so embarrassed. That's when we started making Sunday a Blockbuster night."

has had to make the most adjustments. "This is my dream, not what my husband signed up for," she says. "He's very outgoing and has lots of friends, and, you know, he can't just have them over to watch sports." But it seems Glynn handled the situation just fine. "She'd sometimes entertain the guests with a little dance or a singing show," says Monique. "She's learned how to walk into a room and just own it. Living in this environment has made her very extroverted." As the business grew, so did Glynn, who assumed some of the responsibilities. "She started doing the evening turndown, running baths, sprinkling rose petals," says Monique. By the time she reached her late teens, she'd become the perfect concierge, recommending local restaurants and explaining the subway to guests.

OVER THE YEARS, MONIQUE HAS EXPANDED HER BUSINESS, AND SHE NOW HAS FIVE INNS IN FOUR CITIES (the original Brooklyn location; two in Cape May, N.J.; one in Washington,

Opposite, from top: A portrait of poet Langston Hughes in the D.C. inn. A bedroom in one of the Cape May inns. The living room in Brooklyn.

Above: Glynn and her parents smile on the steps of Akwaaba Mansion in Brooklyn.

D.C.; and one in New Orleans). She and her family have remained at the Brooklyn inn, relying on hired managers to run the offshoots. But she does travel to the other inns to check in occasionally, which is why she and her husband were very careful when choosing where to open each location. "We made sure everything is in alignment," Monique explains. "We chose a city we loved for each season of the year. And now we have a place to stay in those cities."

✳**MELTING POT** "I only have one life. It's not a work life and a home life—it has to come together. I don't just go into a black hole for eight hours. So I've never been afraid to hang my daughter's artwork in my office, and I'm also not afraid to share my home with my work."

Rachel McPherson

THE GOOD DOG FOUNDATION: THERAPY DOG SERVICES

New York, New York
thegooddogfoundation.org

Rachel McPherson was an Academy Award–nominated filmmaker whose dream of someday taking home a golden statue went to the dogs—literally. Married with two kids, she converted the top floor of her Brooklyn townhouse to an office and dog training facility, and started the Good Dog Foundation, a nonprofit that provides therapy dog services to people in need and promotes awareness of the benefits of the human–animal bond. Her decision has been a win all around: She's helping people and animals, and has raised her children to be passionate, caring adults.

IN BUSINESS, PEOPLE ALWAYS SAY THAT THE KEY TO SUCCESS IS THIS: LOOK FOR A NEED, AND FILL IT. They're usually talking about a product that will produce revenue. But Rachel saw a need that wasn't about making money—it was about humanity. She had been an independent filmmaker for many years, and in 1998 was working on her next project, a documentary about animal-assisted therapy. Through her research for the film, she learned something that didn't sit well with her: It was against the law in New York State to bring an animal into a major medical facility, even for therapy purposes. She finished the film and set out to change that.

"I knew that my calling wasn't to make a film about the work," she says. "It was much deeper. The foundation had to be created." Rachel set out to get legislation passed in New York to allow therapy dogs into medical facilities. She worked tirelessly to spread awareness, and started providing training to dog owners and their pets—after 10 classes, the human–dog teams become certified. Now her volunteers help out people in 194 facilities, including assisted-living facilities, schools—and yes, hospitals.

When she started, her kids were 10 and 6, and she saw the endeavor as a bonus to them as well. "I was traveling a lot in my film career, and my husband travels for work too. I didn't want my kids to have two parents on the road. I figured having my office at home would give me more flexibility and I could be there faster, and

✳BALANCING ACT

"The biggest sacrifice I had to make was not picking my kids up from school. That was very emotional for me. But it would have taken two hours out of my workday, so I made a choice. I knew it was more important for me to get my work done so I could be with them when they arrived home, for dinner, and after dinnertime. I was always there during those times."

Above: A Good Dog therapy team consists of an adult volunteer and his or her dog—trained together to help humans heal.

FOR RACHEL, STARTING THE COMPANY WHEN HER KIDS WERE YOUNG WAS KEY, ENABLING THEM TO MATURE ALONG WITH THE BUSINESS. As her organization grew from just a few dogs to more than 700 human–dog teams, it required more of a commitment. "I think it was good to have a startup when the children were younger," she says. "As the company grows, it takes more of my time. But the kids are getting older too, and they're busier with activities and friends. So it's worked out." Now 21 and 17 respectively, Pace and Izzy are totally on board with her mission. "They've always helped out—filing, taking messages, running errands, and training our own dogs,"

more often, for my children." It worked out pretty much exactly as she had hoped. She'd take her kids to school in the morning and go upstairs to work in her office. After school, a nanny would pick up the kids and take them to any activities they needed to get to, and Rachel would step back in at dinnertime. When the kids were home, she didn't exclude them from her day. She'd happily bounce back and forth between Good Dog and family needs. "I could always go downstairs so as not to miss an experience, such as gerbils running in a homemade block maze down the hallway," she says. "And I was there to personally deal with stitches and temperatures."

Top left and above: Hugs are absolutely permitted: Warm, cuddly, and endlessly patient therapy dogs bring solace and smiles to patients in hospitals and nursing homes.

✳**HOW THE KIDS SEE IT** "I believe in my mom's foundation and will help her in any way I can—distributing brochures, training, answering phones, raising money at bake sales. She's taught me that you *can* have both worlds, and now I have an extreme desire to become a successful woman. I want to run my own company one day!"

—**Izzy, 17**

she says. "And now they really get what I'm doing and really support my career. They're both big dog lovers and are very concerned about animals and our environment as a result of being around my work. I know it has had an influence on them."

It's been more than 10 years since Rachel started Good Dog, and it's gotten to the point where the foundation and its administrative staff has outgrown the townhouse. She's moved the facility to an out-of-home space—just as her kids are moving out of the house. Pace is in college, and Izzy will be leaving in a year. The synchronicity has not gone unnoticed by Rachel. "I made a

Above: Rachel lives in Brooklyn, with her husband, two children, three dogs (including one Good Dog) and a rabbit.

choice 11 years ago, and it's been very successful," she reflects. "The timing was just right."

✳**STOP TO SMELL THE ROSES** "You have to savor every moment you have with your kids. The first 15 years of their lives fly by. I learned how important it is to stop what you're doing and help them whenever they need it. I always made a point to stop working when they got home from school to talk to them about their day."

Saras Chung

NEST: BUSINESS SUPPORT FOR FEMALE ARTISANS IN DEVELOPING COUNTRIES

St. Louis, Missouri
buildanest.com

Shortly after receiving a master's degree in social work in 2006, Saras Chung gave birth to her daughter, Karis. It was a happy time, but it was scary too: Karis was born two months early, weighed just three pounds, and was in the NICU at the local hospital. While frightening, the ordeal made Saras realize how lucky she was to live in a prosperous country, with doctors she knew would make sure her baby was okay. So many women around the world aren't so lucky, she thought. Just at that time, her friend Rachel Kousky approached her with an idea: She wanted to start an organization that would help impoverished women around the world to help themselves through social entrepreneurship. The two set about making this happen.

SARAS FELT RACHEL'S IDEA TO ASSIST WOMEN WHO WERE LIVING IN DIRE POVERTY WAS SERENDIPITOUS. Though Karis's premature birth gave Saras and her husband a lot to worry about, Karis was in a hospital in one of the wealthiest countries in the world, and she was healthy. "I had little fear about her survival. I thought about how this would not be the case for many women in other countries." When Rachel explained her plan to establish a nonprofit enterprise that would provide interest-free loans to women artisans and then sell the wares they made, thus enabling the loans to be repaid, "It seemed too good to be true," Saras says. "Helping these women sustain themselves and their families—it was very close to my heart."

The name for the enterprise came easily: Nest. "A shelter or place of refuge in which a mother holds and rears her young—it was perfect," says Saras. For the next few months, she spent her days at the hospital with Karis and then went home to research women and poverty in developing countries. She learned there is an increased risk of premature birth in countries with extremely high poverty rates, and this confirmed that she'd made the right decision to help Rachel with Nest. By the time the organization got off the ground, Karis was home, and Saras set up an office in a spare room next to her bedroom and began the juggling act. Her

Above: In addition to the online business, Nest wares are carried by a number of specialty stores nationwide. Invitational events like this one offer another sales venue.

✴**BALANCING ACT** "I watch my son try to play with his trains while he's eating dinner, and the trains get covered in food and his dinner gets only half eaten. It's better to separate the two. Let playtime be playtime and dinnertime be dinnertime. I think maybe if I had been more deliberate about making clear boundaries between family time and work time, there would be fewer edits to documents!"

✳ **OH NO THEY DIDN'T!**

"I was always careful to keep product inventory stored far out of reach from my kids. One day, however, I walked into the living room to find my 2-year-old daughter with the lid to a Tanzanian basket on her head, singing 'Happy Birthday to You.' Apparently, she thought the lid was a birthday hat. It was a moment when I wanted to scold her for getting into Mommy's stuff, but I just had to laugh."

husband works from home too, so they'd take turns working and tending to Karis. Less than two years later, they had another baby, a son.

"I NAIVELY THOUGHT I COULD GET MY WORK DONE IN THE OFFICE, BUT THE REALITY WAS MY LAPTOP TRAVELED WITH ME FROM ROOM TO ROOM, wherever my kids were working on art projects or playing," she says. Once again, she thought of the women she was helping through Nest. "Thomas the Tank Engine toys everywhere make walking down the hallway to get inventory an adventurous trip," she jokes. "But I imagine the women we help halfway around the globe operate the same way—dodging their children's belongings while working from home to help create a livelihood for their family."

Saras now works for another nonprofit organization but remains close to Rebecca and continues to play an advisory role at Nest. In the three full-time years she spent with Nest, she says she adjusted to working around her kids. She learned to balance work and family by getting major chunks of her work done while the kids were napping or in bed for the night, and

Opposite: As a 2-year-old, Saras' daughter Karis determined that this Nest basket was designed as a wearable.

This page: Nest offers an impressive and constantly changing variety of products, including home accessories and wearables. Many are designed by the women who make them, often in traditional styles and techniques. Nest also connects the artisans with designers in the States who need skilled production help; they, in turn, donate a portion of their sales to Nest.

doing small tasks like sending e-mails when they were awake. With her husband at home, though, there were other options. "When I urgently needed to get something done, my husband would give me the day to go to the library or a coffee shop so I was uninterrupted, and I did the same for him." She often took the children with her in the car when she had to drop off packages or go check out a new T-shirt design for approval.

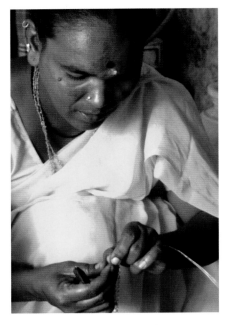

AS THEY GROW OLDER, SARAS PLANS TO GIVE HER KIDS SIMPLE TASKS THAT WILL MAKE THEM FEEL THEY ARE PART OF HER ENDEAVORS. "Helping others in need, compassion, and global awareness are all important things to enmesh into their being," she says. "I especially want to involve my daughter. Coming from a traditional Korean-American background, I was taught that women stay on the sidelines and support the work of men. I want to involve her with Nest so she grows up knowing that there are no boundaries to what she can do. Seeing the Nest women around the world working hard to create a stable life for their families will hopefully inspire her to live beyond herself."

As Saras works on balancing an increasingly complex life, Nest

continues to grow. The organization now works with women in countries like Morocco, Tanzania, India, and Guatemala, helping the artisans to sell their wares online. Perhaps her biggest regret is that she was never able to meet those women since, with two small children at home, she was not willing to travel for work. "Rebecca took care of those trips because she was more able to go than

Opposite: Among the necklaces Nest offers are beads strung on wire links—a task done methodically by hand—with lovely results and international appeal.

Above: Saras and her husband do not let work get in the way of fun with their lively toddlers.

I was," says Saras. "Not being able to meet the women face to face was one of the hardest things about my job. But hopefully, now that the kids are getting older, I'll be able to take a trip someday to meet these women."

✳**A LITTLE GOES A LONG WAY** "Never allow your work to get in the way of your family's happiness. If you're strained in your family life, it will come back to hit you in the face and you won't have the strength to be effective at work. All it might take is one evening out with your family or spouse, but make sure you do it."

Amy Grey

BACKYARD HARVEST: PROVIDES LOCALLY GROWN PRODUCE TO THE NEEDY

Moscow, Idaho
backyardharvest.org

When Amy Grey's sons were 5 and 2, in 2006, they loved being outside and playing in the dirt. She had some space in her backyard, so she started a little vegetable garden. The tiny garden fit the bill and kept them busy. Unwittingly, Amy grew more produce than she knew what to do with. When she gave it to a local food bank, she discovered her donation was the first of its kind. Now her boys are busier than they ever could have hoped to be (and so is Amy), as the garden has become the center of Backyard Harvest, a nonprofit, multi-city project that provides locally grown food to people in need.

AMY GREY WAS NOT A FARMER. She was a free-lance book designer with two rowdy boys in want of entertaining. When she decided to start that first garden to keep Tom and Sam busy, they helped her plant seeds and then tended the plot each day. They were happy, and that made Amy happy. Six weeks later, the results, a surprise crop of 200 heads of lettuce, led them to the local food bank, where Amy took notice of all the food lining the shelves. While she thought it great that so many people were donating food, she felt sad that it was all canned and packaged. "My lettuce was the only fresh thing there," she said. "I realized that so many of my neighbors had really limited access

Below: Never leery of getting their hands dirty, Amy's boys are big-time garden assistants. Here Sam totes water to some thirsty plants.

✳**BALANCING ACT**

"This year, we're holding a big harvest party in October, so community members can see the garden and our office space first hand. It's exciting! Really, having everything happen in my backyard makes it possible to easily combine work and raising two young boys—and four chickens, one bunny, three cats, two mice, and one very understanding husband!"

the backyard harvest

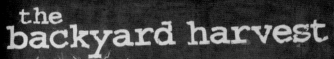

4,019 lbs   **14** doz

of produce collected and distributed
to 20 area foodbanks + meal programs in
moscow, pullman, colfax, troy, kendrick + lewiston

please
drop off
produce
in cart

save the date
ANNUAL HARVEST CELEBRATION OCT 3rd
6PM - HERE !!

to fresh food." The seed for Backyard Harvest was planted.

Amy went home and, with her boys, planted entire packets of various vegetables with the intention to donate the yield to the food bank. Then her friends joined in the cause. "My friends started adding their extra zucchinis to my deliveries, and so on, and it occurred to me that there might be a larger project here," she says. So she came up with a name—Backyard Harvest—and a logo, and found a partner to pilot the project. A few years later, she branched out on her own. Now Backyard Harvest

✳**OH NO THEY DIDN'T!** "There are so many vignettes I can think of. But the one that immediately comes to mind is Sam emerging from the cherry orchard when he was 3 or so. He likes to eat cherries. He came out covered in cherry juice from top to bottom, and poured a grand total of three cherries out of his bucket into the crate!"

Opposite: Amy posts news on a chalkboard at the drop-off shed in her yard, including a tally of produce distributed to "green" food banks.

Above: Amy orchestrates harvest labors at a local apple orchard, and weighs in the bounty.

has locally run chapters in six different cities and a Web site where like-minded people can find information on joining or starting a chapter.

BACKYARD HARVEST HAS BEEN THE PERFECT FIT FOR AMY'S FAMILY. The harvest shed, office, and garden—which has gone from "tiny" to 1,600 square feet—are all at her home, so she spends every day with her sons. The boys, in turn, are happier than pigs in mud. They have endless opportunities to play outside in the dirt: They water the plant starts, clean and organize pots, bag produce, weed, water, harvest—you name it. Of course, there are times when Amy needs a break from it all. "There have unquestionably been days that I am trying to juggle 10 different things and the boys are full of questions and demands and I just want to lock myself away for a couple of hours

✳**HOW THE KIDS SEE IT** "Running around making drop-offs at food banks with my mom can get boring, so I always make sure I bring a good book. But I love being able to pick fruit off the trees and eat it. My favorite orchard is at this stable with horses. The horses have such big, innocent eyes that I keep feeding them the apples in my bucket."

—Tom, 9

of peace and quiet," she says. But those times are few and far between, and the benefits far outweigh the rare moments she considers cons. "Financially," she adds, "we're now in a position to consider a separate location. But I like things the way they are. As a family, we have gotten used to and look forward to neighbors coming by to drop off produce, and having staff and volunteers gather equipment to head out to pick."

"Backyard simply would not have occurred if I had not been a slightly frazzled mother of two young boys, looking for something we could all do together," she says. "The garden has become a great place where we can come together as a family. We've met wonderful people and visited beautiful spots along the way. Picking fruit straight off the tree,

Opposite: Amy's garden is tidy—making it easy to tend and productive, and very pretty.

Above: No one said gardening isn't hard work: Tom, Sam, and Amy enjoy an occasional break.

playing with people's kittens, horses, chickens, and dogs, and generally getting filthy. What more could two energy-filled boys ask for?"

✳**YOU REAP WHAT YOU SOW** "Having the idea for this project was one thing, but actually undertaking it was a little scary. I'd always had clients, and now I was setting out to run my own thing. But I always think about this quote my father has over his desk: 'The cavalry is not coming.' Basically, it means you can't sit around waiting for someone else to make the world a better place. I couldn't be happier with my decision to start this, and the way my life has turned out because of it. I only wish I had attempted all of this much earlier!"

2

A Business Mother's Workshop

The First Steps

The women in this book started their businesses for a variety of reasons. Some wanted to leave their 9-to-5 jobs and work at home so they could spend more time with their families. Others were stay-at-home moms who needed to do something to bring in more money. And many simply had a passion that they could no longer ignore—and they turned that passion into a moneymaking business. Whatever motivates you to begin your business, the first step is to make sure you're prepared. That means, of course, having an idea—what kind of business do you want to launch?—and schooling yourself in the basics, like financing, product development, marketing, and staffing. But it also means making sure you're prepared for how the business will affect your home life. If you think through what's to come and set the right parameters beforehand, you can achieve the professional success and personal fulfillment that the women profiled in this book have found.

DEFINE YOUR BUSINESS

So what do you want to do? Nothing can happen until you have an idea. Perhaps you've always had a particular passion, a talent you've tapped only as a hobby, as Yolanda Owens did when she turned her love of creating her own skin care products into iwi fresh. Or you've discovered a niche that's screaming to be filled, as Rachel McPherson did when she learned of the benefits of therapy dogs and set out to share her discovery. The point is, if you have a passion for something it can become a successful business if you want it to. Never worry that your idea isn't good enough. Barbara Schriber realized that after fretting that no one would buy her gift cards, and finding out she was wrong. "There is a market for everything," she says. "You just have to find your niche—put all of your energy into discovering who your market is. As long as you think it's fab, there *are* others who will think so too."

Once you have an idea, it's time to do your homework. There's a lot to research about the basics of business operation: financing, product development, marketing and sales, staffing, business plans. You also want to consider how the business will fit into your family life: Will you work from your home or lease commercial space? How will you carve out your day? What are the options for help with childcare, in your community and among your family members?

What kinds of boundaries will you set between work life and home life? There are many great resources out there to help you with the basics. The Small Business Administration is a good place to start (as are your local library and the Internet), and

there are other resources listed in the back of this book where you can find more detailed information on topics like marketing and staffing. The rest of this particular workshop focuses on the aspects of launching a business that are especially relevant to mothers striving to achieve a good balance between work and family.

BE READY FOR THE BENEFITS AND THE CHALLENGES

As you've learned from reading the stories of the women in this book, running your own business can be immensely rewarding. Being your own boss gives you more flexibility to break away for your son's soccer game or take your daughter to the dentist, and you have the satisfaction of working for yourself and doing what you love. But there are challenges too. For many of the profiled women, the emotional pull between family and business was something they didn't foresee. Some of those who work at home struggled with guilt over being home yet not actually with their kids. Others found that when they were spending time with their family, the needs of the business were often still present in their mind. Knowing what to expect will make it easier to balance work and family life,

THE INSIDE TRACK

DIANE ALLISON-STROUD, GAME BOARD DESIGNER: "I'm confident in knowing that if I hit a hurdle, I'll figure out a way to overcome it. If I'd actually thought about all of the problems that could arise, I would have scared myself into not trying."

JENNIFER LIST, CHILDREN'S CLOTHING DESIGNER: "Of course there were fears: Would we even get accepted into any of the jury shows? And if we did, would we sell anything? Would people get it? We believed in our products. If we didn't, we wouldn't have even tried."

CARRIE RAPHAEL, INTERIOR DESIGNER: "You need to have an honest conversation with yourself before you start. 'Am I willing to possibly not succeed financially in a grand way as long as I'm doing what I love?' If you commit to going forward, don't second-guess yourself if you slip or fall. You'll just learn a better way to do it next time."

RACHEL MCPHERSON, THERAPY DOG TRAINER: "I just had a calling and knew I had to go with my gut instinct. I wasn't nervous; I've always been driven and determined to overcome challenges. My mother always encouraged me to explore and to tackle difficult situations and not

and later in this book you'll find tips to create boundaries that work for you. The resources in the back of this book also list a number of organizations, books, magazines, and Web sites dedicated to the experiences and needs of women entrepreneurs.

The best approach to combining motherhood and business ownership: Prepare well and don't let the challenges discourage you. Goat cheese producer Tasia Malakasis advises: "You can't let obstacles in front of you become a dark cloud and think, 'I just made the biggest mistake of my life.' I'm a zealot when it comes to being optimistic and positive. The biggest thing is to be confident." All of the women in this book overcame the hurdles they encountered. In fact, they stress that being an entrepreneur doesn't necessarily take any more time away from family than doing any other job. And in the end, they all say the benefits of having a business far outweigh any bumps you may hit give up. My father's dad died when my dad was 3, leaving his mother to support the family, so he knew firsthand the importance of women having a professional life. He was very insistent that I achieve that."

SARAS CHUNG, NONPROFIT FOUNDER: "My baby was a preemie. I was told she would be fine, but I couldn't stop worrying. Starting the nonprofit was a great relief; it helped me get my mind off worrying whether my daughter would grow and develop at the pace she should."

LAURIE LENFESTEY, HANDMADE GOODS PRODUCER: "For some reason, I wasn't at all nervous about how things would go. Ignorance is bliss!"

ZHENA MUZYKA, TEA MAKER: "To create something from a vision is not easy, but the first step is the most difficult—it requires you to be brave. Abandon your fear of failure to create something beautiful in the world."

JEN O'CONNOR, FOLK-ARTISTS' REP: "I questioned my ability a little— but I more questioned my right to do what I wanted. I had to remind myself that worrying takes time and accomplishes nothing."

MARYELLEN KIM, ACCESSORIES AND HOME GOODS PRODUCER: "When it finally sank in that people liked my work, and would be willing to pay a fair price for me to make it, I was thrilled. The rest is history."

along the way. Says chandelier creator Meredith Clark: "I try to picture what life would be like if I had a run-of-the-mill day job. Honestly, I think so many of the questions of balance would still be there. What would be missing, though, would be the incredible opportunity I have had to work while essentially being a stay-at-home mom. I've been able to share my creativity, my process, my confidence, my faith, my failures, my successes, and my dreams with my children." Echoes Backyard Harvest founder Amy Grey: "I have not regretted a moment of the journey I am on. Despite the long hours and all of the hard work, it is so much fun and there are enormous advantages like a flexible schedule. My only regret is that I didn't attempt this much earlier in my life!"

TALK TO YOUR FAMILY

Just as important as knowing what's to come is making sure to keep your family in the loop. Communication is key to avoiding disappointment later on. If you're planning to work from home, for example, your kids need to know that while you'll be home, it doesn't mean you'll be able to hang out with them all the time—or even most of the time. Explain things clearly so everyone knows what to expect. If your kids are old enough, have a frank conversation with them about how things might change, and find out what's important to them. You may not think they care whether you or a nanny picks them up from school, but have you ever actually asked them? Now's the time.

Asking them which aspects of you as a mom are most important to them will help you plan how to divide your time. Revisit these conversations from time to time as your kids and your business grow. And don't forget to include your husband in these discussions. Says inn owner Monique Greenwood: "I didn't realize that sitting down to dinner as a family means the world to my husband. I would have focused more on making that happen if I had known! Definitely have conversations with your whole family before you start, to find out what's important to everyone."

Your Business Plan

As legendary entrepreneur T. Boone Pickens once said, "A fool with a plan can outsmart a genius without a plan." If you're a genius with a plan, imagine how far you'll go! Once you've established what you're going to do, and have prepared yourself and your family for the journey, it's time to write your business plan. This may sound very corporate, but basically a business plan is just a road map to a destination—in other words, a list of the steps you need to take to achieve your goals. There are many resources available to help you. Some tips are listed here, and there are templates to be found online and in the library. Going through the process of developing a business plan will force you to think through the requirements of your business and make it less likely you'll encounter major unexpected situations later.

DO SOME RESEARCH FIRST

Before you start crafting your plan, do your homework. Knowledge of your business—or lack of it—can make the difference between success and failure. Cheryl A. Mills, associate deputy administrator of Entrepreneurial Development for the U.S. Small Business Administration (SBA), urges every potential entrepreneur to become educated about her dream business and the steps for making it happen. She stresses four key points to research:

THE MARKET: Learn about the market for your particular goods or services:

BUSINESS PLAN CHECKLIST

- Define your business clearly so you can articulate it succinctly.

- Research the components of an effective business plan; learn everything you can about your market; do realistic financial planning.

- Write the plan yourself—this is the best way to learn what you need to know to be true to your vision and prepared to "open your doors."

- Take advantage of consultants; you needn't (and probably won't be able to) figure it all out for yourself.

- Give it a professional format that reflects your commitment: Include a table of contents and an executive summary so an overview is readily accessible. Type it neatly and bind it (inexpensive binding is fine).

THE BUSINESS OF YOUR BUSINESS: Learn how to put together a solid business plan and figure out how you'll manage the business itself.

THE MONEY: Research how much financing you'll need and the options for putting it together.

EXPERT HELP: There are numerous resources available to help you develop your plan; take advantage of them. Good starting places include the SBA, the Women's Business Center, and SCORE: Counselors to America's Small Business. There are many other sources offering advice; find out what and where they are (see resources on page 184 of this book to get started). Don't forget to talk to your friends and other contacts, and use the Internet and library to learn as much as you can.

WRITE—AND REWRITE

All business plans cover basically the same principles (see Five Essentials for Every Business Plan, page 166). When you're ready to actually start writing, an Internet search or a visit to your local library or office-supply store will turn up templates galore. Remember to be true to yourself and your vision. At the same time, be sure to stay realistic

Who are your potential customers, what are their interests and how does your idea serve them? Then learn how to meet your customers' needs: What makes your business unique and how will you reach the customer?

AMY BARICKMAN, FABRIC ARTS PRODUCER: "Failing to plan is planning to fail. Believe me, I need this advice daily! You must put a plan in place. Find someone to help you and put together a mini board of directors (business owners you know) to review it. Then, along the way, make sure you take time to review it. Sometimes things change—for example, an economic downturn—that require you to re-examine the plan and tweak it."

MARYELLEN KIM, ACCESSORIES AND HOME GOODS PRODUCER: "A business plan is totally necessary if you are seeking financing from a bank or investors. But even if you're not, you need one. For me, it's about focusing on what I want my business to be. The process has helped me realize what is important to me within the business and how to achieve my goals. And referring back to it helps keep me from getting distracted by all of the extraneous tasks and issues that come about."

HEIDI CHAPMAN, GIFT STORE OWNER: "I researched what was going on economically before I decided on where to open my store. I didn't want my business to depend on the local economy, so I chose to open my first store off the highway, away from the downtown area. There were a lot of naysayers, but I'd done my research—and it turned out to be a good decision. I've seen at least five retail stores open downtown since I opened, and they've all gone out of business."

MEREDITH CLARK, CHANDELIER CREATOR: "I used to operate without a business plan. Now that I have one, I find it extremely helpful. It has been a great learning experience to sit down and write out both what has been done in the past and what I would like to see in the future. When they're on paper and articulated, goals are able to take form and be manifest."

SERENA THOMPSON, ANTIQUES SHOW PRODUCER: "Any business decision that doesn't feel like it is a good fit for my family, I won't do it."

and conservative with your financial forecasts—if you do better than anticipated, you'll look stellar.

Once you've completed a draft, solicit feedback from a number of people whose opinion you respect.

FIVE ESSENTIALS FOR EVERY BUSINESS PLAN

1. Begin with a statement of purpose. You should be able to explain your business in 25 words or less.

2. Tell how your business will work and why it will be successful. List the owners.

3. Fill in the business details. Describe its products or services, the customers, the market, and the competition. List the managers and their credentials.

4. Supply three years of projected financial statements. Include income, loss, and cash-flow projections.

5. Provide supporting documents, such as references from creditors and potential clients and suppliers, evidence of insurance, etc.

SCORE: Counselors to America's Small Business
Washington, D.C.

Bring your plan to one of the many Small Business Association offices, where experienced advisers are available to give you an objective assessment of your proposal. Gift store owner Heidi Chapman suggests checking with your local Chamber of Commerce. "Many of them offer expertise in this area, with a group of retired businesspeople who are very willing to help," she says. And be resourceful! When Chapman was getting ready to launch her retail company, she contacted wholesale giants AmericasMart and the Dallas Market Center and asked whether they offered retail consulting services.

Don't take anything personally. You cannot get so attached to your plan that you fail to acknowledge its shortcomings or allow yourself to recognize and seize opportunities that may come along. Keep an eye on the future and heed the feedback you receive!

Financing

As you developed your business plan, you probably touched on the idea of money—how much you'll need and where it will come from. You'll need initial startup capital, and an idea of the cash flow or reserves needed to keep your business afloat. Talk to your accountant to come up with a plan that works for you. You might be in a position to secure investors or a business loan to get your business off the ground. Or you may choose to develop your business slowly, using personal savings or gifts from family and friends.

BUSINESS LOANS AND CREDIT CARDS

There are a number of sources for debt financing—credit cards, bank loans, and government agencies such as the Small Business Administration. Check into what's available for you, but be cautious not to bite off more than you can chew. Consider the overall economic conditions: When things are booming, borrowing may be a good option, but during a downturn, even if you are approved for a loan or credit card, you will probably be slapped with high interest rates that can be difficult for a new business to keep up with. The

upside? If you can keep up with the payments, it will put you in a good light should you need to borrow more in the future. Make sure you understand your personal liability for any business loans you accept.

INVESTORS

If you have prepared your business plan properly and can present it with passion, you may be able to persuade investors to join your cause. Before you approach them, invest some of your own money to show that you truly believe your idea is worthy of risk. Finding investors means sharing your idea with everyone

---

FINANCING CHECKLIST

- Your business plan should spell out the amount of capital you need to launch. A rule of thumb is enough to cover a year's operating expenses, but that may be more than needed—it depends on the nature of your business.

- Take advantage of Small Business Administration counseling. Explore the types of financing available. Determine which type is right for you.

- Consult a certified public accountant to be sure your plans are appropriate and realistic.

- Talk to potential lenders, be they bank officials, friends, or family. Sell them the idea of your business.

- Invest personal savings if you have them—this signals you believe in your plan and are making a serious commitment to its success.

---

you know. Talk to friends and friends of friends, and approach the SBA for potential investors.

GROW SLOWLY, BUT BE CREATIVE

It's understandable to be cautious about borrowing money. Between the unknowns of a new business and unpredictable overall economic conditions, you may not have the confidence that you'll be successful enough to pay back loans—or to return a profit to investors. Most of the women profiled in this book suggest the best way to begin is to go the grassroots route and develop your business slowly, using money you already have. Keeping your overhead at a minimum may mean working out of your home until you are sure you can swing rent elsewhere, putting in some major hours to avoid having to hire help, and coming up with creative ways to get the basics you'll need to begin. Before Libby Wienke could launch her design company, she needed supplies to make prototypes to show to potential clients. She practiced patience, using holidays to build up her tool kit. "I asked for gift certificates to hardware, hobby, and fabric stores for my birthday and Christmas," she says. Saras Chung found pro-bono lawyers to give her

THE INSIDE TRACK

YOLANDA OWENS, NATURAL SKIN CARE PRODUCTS CREATOR: "You need money to get money, and luckily I had enough success from my time in corporate America to create a foundation for my business. It was enough to get family members and friends excited about my business, and later I received donations from them."

AMY BARICKMAN, FABRIC ARTS PRODUCER: "Be very aware of cash flow, and stay involved in reviewing your financial details each month. It is much better to be in a proactive situation than a reactive one."

DIANE ALLISON-STROUD, GAME BOARD DESIGNER: "When you overlap your business with your personal finances, you're always robbing Peter to pay Paul. It's a week of steak or a week of pasta. I've found it's best to take a percentage off of each paycheck and put it back into the business account. This way, I always have cash flow—money to buy supplies and pay advertising fees."

MARYELLEN KIM, ACCESSORIES AND HOME GOODS PRODUCER: "I wanted to do all the books myself and not have the cost of an accountant, but while QuickBooks is a great tool, it can be very complicated. I hired an accountant with expertise in the software to come out and set up the program specifically for my type of business. It has turned out to be a great compromise between hiring a professional accountant and doing it all myself."

BARBARA SCHRIBER, GIFT CARD AND WRAPPING PAPER DESIGNER: "In late 2008 when the economy really took a dive, I resurrected my company on a limited basis. Extra money is nice. Don't walk away from extra money—that's something I've learned in this economy."

advice when launching her nonprofit, Nest. She and her partner also sought help from their alma mater—and their resourcefulness resulted in free money. "We applied for a grant from our university and ended up winning $30,000, which maintained Nest for the first two years," she says.

QUESTIONS TO ASK YOUR ACCOUNTANT

- Do I have enough money? Don't enter into any legal, binding agreements or make investment decisions you cannot afford.

- Which business entity best suits my new business venture: a sole proprietorship, corporation, S-corporation, partnership, or limited liability company (LLC)?

- Which taxes and insurances must I plan for? Income taxes are just the beginning; there are also sales and use taxes, payroll taxes, workers' compensation insurance, disability insurance, liability insurance, and more.

- What are proper bookkeeping techniques? A good accountant can help set up a system that works best for you, an essential for successful business management.

Janice Yahr, CPA
Yahr & Lally
Ronkonkoma, New York

Space and Boundaries

Where your business is going to live and breathe is something you should have decided when crafting your business plan. If you're going to invest in a commercial location, you would have factored that into your budget. And if your plan is to work at your home, there are other issues to consider: Do you have the space? How will you ensure that your kids respect your workspace and the space of your staff? Most of the women in this book started their businesses at home and offered advice on how to make that work. But keep in mind that as your business grows, it will likely outgrow your home—whether it's products overtaking every room in your house, or the emotional pull of housing two aspects of your life in one physical space. Be ready to make the change before the business becomes a burden to your family.

IN-HOME BUSINESSES

Running your business from your home no doubt keeps overhead low. It also gives you the ability to be there with or for your kids, if you have small children not in school yet, or grade-schoolers home in the late afternoon. However, even if you have a full-time nanny taking care of them while you work, don't expect that your kids will always respect the business owner-mom boundary.

Many of the moms in this book decided to go with an open door policy, allowing the little ones to draw and paint while Mom worked in the same room. And for some, having their kids right there serves as inspiration—as when Libby Wienke's daughter made a drawing Libby thought would make a great motif on a fabric. "I saw this lizard she drew and decided to borrow it," says Libby. "I scanned the face and used it on a printed dinosaur-themed bedding set." She also enlisted her daughter to draw the numbers for a hopscotch rug she created, and has asked both of her kids to test her products.

Another good way to keep the kids busy while you work is to give them tasks to do. This need not go to the extent of using their drawings on your product; small duties like sorting, stuffing envelopes, or applying stamps to mailings are often enough to keep kids busy and entertained. And, say many of the women, welcoming the kids into the workspace sparked unexpected creativity. "I picked my son Dante up from pre-school one day and he led me over to a Lite Brite he had been playing with," remembers Meredith Clark. "'Look, Mom!' he beamed. 'It's a new chandelier design I did! Isn't it cool?' I was amazed to realize how much he understood about what I did, and how much he appreciated the work I do." As your kids get older, they may or may not take an interest in your business. Monique Greenwood's daughter, Glynn, was only 3 when

Monique opened her first bed and breakfast. Now a teenager, Glynn is benefiting from having an automatic apprenticeship in her mother's business. "She's decided that she wants to pursue public relations and marketing," says Monique of her daughter, "so I engage her in what I do to promote Akwaaba."

The bottom line, say the women who are doing it, is that having a business at home comes with both pros and cons. Says Saras Chung: "Keeping things separate is helpful for productivity, but including your kids in certain aspects of your work will help your family grow and broaden their love for others. Having them learn about the work you do will enforce the messages you're trying to instill in them—working hard at what you do, and creating an impact on something that's bigger than yourself."

STAFF IN YOUR HOME

If you have employees working in your home, it's important to remember that when they're present, they are at work. These are *your* kids, not theirs, and you should make sure your kids respect your employees' space and tools. Meredith Clark says this is something she struggles with all the time. She recalls

THE INSIDE TRACK

JENNIFER LIST, CHILDREN'S CLOTHING DESIGNER: "I work whenever and wherever I can fit it in. Slippers have been sewn in hotel rooms, sweaters trimmed on airplanes, and necklaces designed at the beach house. I may be serving more frozen pizza than I used to, but I make a point to carve out time with my family—a day at the beach, a nice vacation."

DIANE ALLISON-STROUD, GAME BOARD DESIGNER: "My boys have been a source of inspiration. I think a lot when I paint. It's peaceful and gives me time to think about my family. Once when Davey was going through some tough teenage years, as all kids do, I was doing a board with a flower in the center. It reminded me of Davey's struggle to find himself, the flower being his center, and the many steps he'd take to find his own center. It was a Parcheesi board that I called 'Davey's Garden.'"

MEREDITH CLARK, CHANDELIER CREATOR: "I have a short cleaning ritual I do daily to transition the space from office to home. I tidy up, play some music, and burn some incense. It's what I do so I feel like I can then give all of my attention to my home and my children."

DEBBIE HAUPT, ANTIQUES MARKET PRODUCER: "When my kids were little, I was working out of my garage. It was easy because I was there when the kids needed me, and I could be busy and creative when they didn't. Then by the time I rented space and moved the business away from our home, my kids were teenagers, so my parenting skills weren't in constant demand."

JEN O'CONNOR, FOLK-ARTISTS' REP: "My workspace is invaluable for organizing art and inventory, planning photo shoots, etc. It's so important that this space is separate from the house. When I was first in the biz, before we built the building, it really made me crazy. Sometimes it was a train wreck—boxes and bins galore. Plus, I work a lot, and having that physical separation helps me to not get to that next task and instead call it quits for the night."

many instances where her colleagues were frustrated by her boys getting into their things. She sends her kids off to "do a lap around the house" when she and her staff are frustrated and need some quiet time. And when an employee needs to get away in order to focus, she respects his or her wishes. "They know when to say, 'I am taking these cost sheets home to work on them there,' or 'I am leaving so I can work on the Web site, uninterrupted,'" says Meredith. This is the flexibility I grant everyone, as a team. I rarely question when an afternoon off is taken, or someone shows up at 9:30 instead of 9."

Of course, choosing the right staff is paramount—especially when they'll be working in your home. The women in this book say their hires mostly came through word of mouth and are people they've known and trusted for years. And if you have employees you care about and respect, they will in turn adapt to having kids around the office and even become like family. "My Chandi team is truly an extension of family for my boys," says Meredith Clark. "Banderas, who has worked with me now for seven years, is like an uncle to them. He sets boundaries as far as his workspace and tools are concerned, and in exchange he respects the fact that this is the home of two young boys who need room to play and discover."

GET OUT OF DODGE!

An overwhelming majority of the women in this book say their ability to separate work and family grew immensely once they moved their business out of their home. Many of them say they would have leased commercial space sooner, if they could have afforded it. So if you have the funding to rent a commercial space from the get-go, it's something worth considering. If you don't, try setting up shop in the garage, barn, or other physical space that isn't a go-to area in your home. Part of your motivation for starting a business may be the ability to stay home with your kids, but if you want your business to be successful, you'll need to be able to focus when you're working. And, as many of these women learned the hard way, that's impossible to do when you're constantly being pulled away from a phone call or a project to, say, check out the four-foot-tall Lego mansion your son just built.

Vicki Mote Bodwell remembers the days when she ran Warm Buscuit Bedding out of her bedroom: "When I was working at home, every day seemed like a race. My boys were both babies and when I wasn't answering phones or organizing photo shoots, I was holding them. Even though I had a sitter, it was impossible for them to play in the other room knowing I was there. And it was hard for me not to run out to see what they were up to throughout the day. Plus, at night, I was always still very aware of work—phone lines would be blinking, faxes would come through, and of course there were the constant reminders, like fabric swatches hanging on the walls and catalogs stacked around the room. Everything was chaotic and messy." Moving her business out of the bedroom, she says, was a "game-changer" for her family.

If you do start out at home, recognize when the line between work and home starts to become too blurred—and start looking for offsite space. Ann Marie Craig has been making soap in her log cabin farmhouse since 2000, mixing it right on her kitchen stove, drying it on the porch, and storing it upstairs. But she knows it's time to push Century Farmhouse out of the nest. The stock often spills out into the living room downstairs, and it's putting a strain on the family. She's currently looking for an off-site space for production. "The story of our soaps has to do with them being created in a farmhouse venue, so it's sad to move the business out," she says. "But at the same time, it has grown to the point where a move is necessary for both business expansion and family sanity."

If you don't have the means to move offsite, or you simply prefer to be at home, well, you may just have to learn to accept the chaos, as Diane Allison-Stroud did for a while. "There was a time when my business took over our living space," recalls Diane, who allowed her work to spill out of her studio while her second child was too young for school. "I was painting on the kitchen table, there were game boards leaning on all of the walls, and everyone was feeling a little cramped. But you just have to go with the flow. I couldn't spend my time fighting a fight I probably wouldn't have won." When Eli started school, she felt more in control and moved back into her studio.

The Work–Family Balance

Whether your business is at home or somewhere else, finding time for both the business and your family is likely to require careful planning. It's the same for any working mother, but when it's your company it can be a little more difficult to find a balance. After all, when your job is *your* baby, and not just something you do for someone else, the emotional attachment is stronger. But, of course, you have your real children who need your time too. So what's the secret to achieving a sustainable work–life balance?

WORK AROUND YOUR FAMILY

If your kids are in school, your work schedule is pretty much set for you. After dropping them off, you'll have the whole day to work while they're not at home. You may stop for the day when they get back or take a brief break to have dinner and help them with homework, tying up any loose ends once they're in bed. But for the women in this book who started out with young children at home, establishing working hours meant fitting in productive time whenever possible.

According to these women, the old adage is true: The early bird catches the worm. "I try to get up earlier than everyone else, to have a cup of coffee outside before squeezing in a few hours of work," says game board designer Diane Allison-Stroud. And apparently, being a night owl isn't out of the question either: "Basically, I spaced my work throughout the times when I wasn't needed by my kids," she says. "In the beginning, it wasn't uncommon to find me painting at 2 a.m." It's a common thread among the women with kids at home: Get up early, sometimes as early as 4:30 a.m., to take advantage of the quiet hours. And be willing to put in extra time late at night.

STAY FOCUSED

You can expect to miss a few dinners (and order a lot of takeout) or to forfeit an occasional baseball game, and in that sense, running your own business is no different from working full time anywhere else. But working 9 to 5 usually means that when you get home you're fully ready to focus on your family. That's not always the case when you're your own boss. You may be home physically, but find yourself mentally slipping into work mode even when you're not actually working. Laurie Lenfestey says trying to raise her kids while starting Bittersweet Designs left her feeling like she was coming up short in both roles: "It's just so hard juggling so many things; you feel like you're never doing any one thing well enough, because your mind is always on both things." Saras Chung shares her sentiment. "It's so easy to get engrossed in either work or family," she says. "It

always seems that one or the other does not get your full attention."

A few things these women have learned along the way: Shut down your computer at a certain time so you're not tempted to check e-mail during non-working hours. When you're out with your kids or husband, turn off your cell phone. Better yet, leave it at home. And try to keep anything that reminds you of work—supplies, logos, correspondence—tucked away so it's out of sight.

CARVE OUT FAMILY TIME

If you find yourself working 18-hour days, or every day of the week, it's time to stop and evaluate. Learn from the profiled women's experiences and start treating your family the way you do meetings: Schedule time to spend with them. It may sound cold and informal, but it will ensure you're not neglecting things at home. Monique Greenwood decided to make Sundays Mom–daughter days. "It was a day just for us, when we'd go to the movies," she says. "I was always so tired, though, inevitably I'd fall asleep in the theater! So we started renting movies. It didn't matter where we were—it was *our* day."

Many of the women say that between work and taking care of the

THE INSIDE TRACK

AMY BARICKMAN, FABRIC ARTS PRODUCER: "One year I was at Quilt Market, and my son and husband came along. My mother was there too; she had come along to babysit Jack during the show. It was Halloween, which was sad because Jack couldn't go trick-or-treating. But he dressed in his tiger costume and we played in the hotel room. We just took photos and had fun."

DIANE ALLISON-STROUD, GAME BOARD DESIGNER: "I think every woman should think about what makes her feel like she's doing a good job for her family and make that task number one. Whether it's having a clean house or making cookies for your kids—pick one thing and focus on it, and everything else will fall into place."

SARAS CHUNG, NONPROFIT FOUNDER: "I don't feel so guilty about working when my kids are playing or doing crafts. And I imagine it will only get better when they get older and have different activities going on. They won't need me as much, and it will get easier."

JEN O'CONNOR, FOLK-ARTISTS' REP: "I don't have a cell phone. That way, when I'm not in my home office, I can't be bothered. It's a pet peeve of mine seeing folks walking around town with their kids and talking on their cell phones."

TASIA MALAKASIS, GOAT CHEESE PRODUCER: "I haven't worried much about not being with my son enough when he's young. Lots of moms decide to take time off from work until their kids are in school. But I think children need their parents in a different way, and maybe more, when they're older. When they're little, they just need to be loved and fed. When they're older, they have stressors and have to make important decisions. They may not know they need you, but they need you. So I think it will be more important for me to figure out how to be at home more later."

kids, their husbands by default took the last spot on their to-do lists. Rachel McPherson, Serena Thompson, and Saras Chung have all learned that scheduling weekly date nights is as important as scheduling meetings. And Rachel says she and her husband stay connected with each other via e-mail or phone calls throughout the day too. For Betz White and her husband, quality time is found when the kids are in bed. "We take an early morning walk together, or have a late evening in front of the TV with snacks," she says. "It's our time just for each other." Even if you work with your partner, it's important to have time together that's not about work. Although Mia Galison shares her New York studio with her husband and is with him all day long, she says they have a ritual: After walking their kids to school, they stroll around Central Park before heading off to work. "It's just a nice way to start the day together," she says.

Vacations—even if they're just short getaways once in a while—are always a great way to strengthen the family bond. "You have to make sure that the breaks you take for your family are quality breaks," says Amy Barickman, who takes a six-week sabbatical every summer and spends time with her family at their cottage in northern Michigan. "You will return to the business rested, revived, and full of joy and energy." Often, running your own business comes with lots of work travel, and there isn't a whole lot of time left for personal vacations. A lot of women say bringing the family along on their work trips kills two birds with one stone. "If I have to be at a conference in, say, Miami, we'll tack on three days and the family will join me," says Monique Greenwood. "My husband will play golf while I'm at the conference, and then when I'm done we'll hang out." Debbie Haupt leaves the kids at home with family once a year and goes on a work trip for her antiques business with her husband. "We take a trip to Europe together every year," she says. "We hit as many flea markets as we can in two weeks, then ship a container of our finds home. It's added another dimension to the business—and given us time to be together doing something we enjoy."

Staying on Track

Even with all of this advice up front, there will probably be moments when you simply feel overwhelmed. The key to getting through those times and moving forward is to remember that any hurdle you might encounter is just that, a hurdle. And hurdles can be overcome—and may even turn out to be a positive in the end. Most important? Don't neglect the person who is juggling it all: *You.*

LESSONS IN DISGUISE

Seeking out as much advice in the beginning, and support throughout your endeavor, will no doubt help things go more smoothly. And remember, even when they don't, you're learning, so that once the rough patch passes, you'll be able to avoid the same thing in the future. Diane Allison-Stroud nearly had a mini meltdown in the early days of her game board company, but she mastered the situation and quickly realized the challenge only bettered her business. "I had an order for more than 200 game boards for a catalog," she recalls. "Part of my finishing process is putting my work out in the sun to dry so it gets a good, hard finish. Well, we were in a front of rain, rain, and more rain for days. I was on a serious deadline, and I was scared. But I found a different finishing technique because of that, and it's one I'm still using today. So whenever a scary time happens now, I try to find something good in it."

Monique Greenwood once found herself in a sticky situation that not only worked out—it was also partly responsible for her inn's huge success. "When I still had a full-time job, I knew I couldn't give inn guests the level of service they'd require if they were coming during the week, because

I had to work. So I had to limit reservations to business folks, who would be coming and leaving the same time I was and wouldn't miss me while I was at work. I'd just tell other people that I was booked during the week. Ironically, it ended up creating a fever pitch, because we seemed so in demand!"

ME TIME

Between your business and your family commitments, it may feel as if there is no time left for yourself. But neglecting yourself is likely to produce a domino effect that will eventually knock down every other piece of your life. If you don't feel good, there's no way you'll be able to put the energy you need to into either your business or your family. So take care of yourself—whatever that means to you. Whether it's a few minutes of meditation, a weekly lunch with your girlfriends, or a quiet walk alone, "me time" should be a non-negotiable item on your schedule.

"You have to stay healthy so you have the energy to take care of your family and your business," confirms Yolanda Owens of iwi fresh. Century Farmhouse owner Ann Marie Craig admits that finding the time isn't easy—which is why she literally blocks out time in her calendar for herself.

"Setting aside personal time is hard," she says. "It tends to get eaten up by all of the little things that need doing when there's no other time for them. I have resorted to actually scheduling in some down time for myself on the calendar—just as I do for my husband." And tea maker Zhena Muzyka finds comfort in small comforts, which she says are crucial to mental stability: "The balance of feeding your soul in the process of feeding everyone else's is the most difficult; when you're needed all around, you tend to forget about yourself. But you need to make sure your cup is filled. Everyone needs you—you have to get to soccer practice, to a meeting, to your iPhone when it's going crazy with e-mails . . . You have to be able to stay calm and give yourself the quiet moments you need. A long, hot bath with a glass of champagne, a cup of tea, meditation—whatever it is, it's non-negotiable. You'll start to short-circuit if you don't." Echoes Libby Wienke: "The risk of burnout is real. When that happens, I find an escape—a book, a pedicure, or a girls' weekend at the lake."

As far as dealing with day-to-day issues, antiques seller Debbie Haupt says that laughter is always the best medicine. Finding little ways to lighten

THE INSIDE TRACK

LIBBY WIENKE, CHILDREN'S PRODUCT DESIGNER: "It's really easy, especially in winter, to feel like the walls are closing in. I mean, I'm home all the time. So sometimes it's important to force yourself to leave—run to the bookstore, go sit in a bakery. Something just to get out of the house."

YOLANDA OWENS, NATURAL SKIN CARE PRODUCTS CREATOR: "Every morning, I get up early and meditate in a special place in my home before my kids are awake. And throughout the day, I take deep breaths every chance I get to slow down."

TASIA MALAKASIS, GOAT CHEESE PRODUCER: "I take care of myself by going to Greece every year. I can't be a whole person unless I do that."

RACHEL MCPHERSON, THERAPY DOG TRAINER: "My time comes in the form of exercise. When the staff takes lunch, I go for a bike ride or a jog. I really believe you should schedule time for exercise every day. It clears your head."

BETZ WHITE, HOME ACCESSORIES DESIGNER: "I have the occasional girls' day out with a friend to hit a flea market or just grab a cup of coffee."

MONIQUE KEEGAN, INTERIOR DESIGNER AND ANTIQUES DEALER: "I have a knitting group that allows me to get together with the girls weekly. I also try to schedule in some pampering time whenever I can."

AMY GREY, LOCAL PRODUCE FOOD BANK FOUNDER: "I got myself a road bike, and I love to go on long rides through the countryside. It's nice during those times when I feel like I want to lock myself away from everything."

BARBARA SCHRIBER, GIFT CARD AND WRAPPING PAPER DESIGNER: "My time is simple: I turn on my iPod and listen to podcasts."

up a tense situation is a piece of advice many of the women are quick to offer. "During a hectic sale, my vendors and I like to do funny things," says Haupt. "We leave silly things in each other's spaces and put really high prices on very ugly things to see if anyone notices. It makes a crazy day more fun." And if it ever starts to feel like you have so much to do that you don't even know where to begin, accessories designer Maryellen Kim says to take a deep breath—and tackle just one thing. "When my list of things to do is a mile long, it's overwhelming and I start to feel paralyzed," she says. "That's when I try to hyper-focus on one thing, and only one. It helps if it's a small and easily accomplished task, like answering just one e-mail. Once I finish that task, it sort of opens me up. Then I pick one more. It's amazing how effective this little mind game can be."

SHARING IDEAS

As you nurture and expand your business, using what you've learned to help women who are just starting out can be a great way to step outside your own professional life. For Libby Wienke, mentoring others has provided a welcome reprieve to her daily routine. "I love my work, but after five years the newness has worn off," she says. "So I've started working with other illustrators and artists, helping them get their ideas into production. Seeing their design processes inspires me—and allows me to sort of have colleagues. It can sometimes feel isolating working for yourself, so I find this to be helpful in so many ways." Maryellen Kim agrees that talking to other women in the same boat is invaluable to her sanity. Reaching out to one another, she says, is the best way to get through the tough times and get closer and closer to achieving the ideal work-life balance. "I talk to women through the Switchboards, Etsy, and other craft media," she says. "They share my pursuits and successes, as well as my challenges. Although many of these women I have never met, they have helped me in countless ways. And hopefully, I've helped them as well."

Resources

MENTOR DIRECTORY

Diane Allison-Stroud
Diane Allison Game Boards
dallison.squarespace.com
(828) 265-0977

Amy Barickman
Indygo Junction Inc.
indygojunction.com
The Vintage Workshop
thevintageworkshop.com
(877) 546-3946

Vicki Mote Bodwell
Warm Biscuit Bedding
warmbiscuit.com
(800) 231-4231

Heidi Chapman
The Cloverleaf
thecloverleafboutique.com
(580) 224-0400

Meredith Clark
Chandi Design
chandidesign.com
(866) 4CHANDI (866 424-2634)

Ann Marie Craig
Century Farmhouse
centuryfarmhouse.com
(262) 334-2321

Mia Galison
eeBoo Corp.
eeboo.com
(212) 222-0823

Monique Greenwood
Akwaaba
akwaaba.com
(866) 466-3855

Amy Grey
Backyard Harvest
backyardharvest.org
(208) 669-2259

Debbie Haupt
Haupt Antiek Market
hauptantiek.com
(651) 329-3871

Monique Keegan
Enjoy Co.
enjoyco.net
(740) 405-1316

Maryellen Kim
Twist Style
twiststyle.com
(804) 530-5146

Laurie Lenfestey
Bittersweet Designs
bittersweetdesigns.com
(505) 660-1953

Jennifer List and Stacy
Waddington
Seven Smooches
sevensmooches.com
(708) 203-3546

Tasia Malakasis
Fromagerie Belle Chèvre
bellechevre.com
(800) 735-2238

Haile McCollum
Fontaine Maury
fontainemaury.com
(229) 226-2952

Rachel McPherson
The Good Dog Foundation
thegooddogfoundation.org
(888) 859-9992

Zhena Muzyka
Zhena's Gypsy Tea
gypsytea.com
(800) 448-0803

Jen O'Connor
Earth Angels Toys
earthangelstoys.com
(845) 986-8720

Yolanda Owens
iwi fresh
iwifresh.com
(888) 200-1860

Jennifer Paganelli
Sis Boom Fabrics
sisboom.com
(203) 761-0442

Carrie Raphael
Raphael Designs
raphaeldesigns.com
(443) 404-9330

Rebecca Rather
Rather Sweet Bakery & Café
rathersweet.com
(830) 990-0498

Barbara Schriber
Barbara Schriber Designs
barbaraschriberdesigns.com
(208) 255-7741

Serena Thompson
The Farm Chicks
thefarmchicks.com
(509) 954-1692

Betz White
Betz White Productions
betzwhite.com

Libby Wienke
Happy Monkey Design
www.happymonkeydesign
.com
(314) 918-7469

BUSINESS RESOURCES

Professional Directory
Cheryl A. Mills, Associate
Deputy Administrator
Office of Entrepreneurial
Development
U.S. Small Business
Administration
409 Third Street SW,
6th floor
Washington, D.C. 20416
www.sba.gov
(202) 401-5004

Mary Schaeffer
Accounts Payable Now &
Tomorrow
560 Peoples Plaza #197
Newark, DE 19702
www.ap-now.com
(302) 836-0540

SCORE: Counselors to
America's Small Business
409 Third Street SW,
6th floor
Washington, D.C. 20024
www.score.org
(800) 634-0245

Janice M. Yahr, CPA
Yahr and Lally
3505 Veterans Memorial
Highway #N
Ronkonkoma, NY 11779
(631) 737-2080

Craft Associations/Trade
Organizations
American Craft Council
72 Spring Street
New York, NY 10012
www.craftcouncil.org/
(212) 274-0630
Membership includes
subscription to *American
Craft Magazine*; reference
library; craft shows

Americans for the Arts
1000 Vermont Avenue NW,
6th floor
Washington, D.C. 20005
(202) 371-2830
New York City Office
One East 53rd Street,
2nd floor
New York, NY 10022
www.artsusa.org
(212) 223-2787
Advocacy and professional
organization

American Society of Interior
Design
608 Massachusetts Avenue
NE
Washington, D.C. 20002
www.asid.org
(202) 546-3480
Professional educational
organization

Apparel Industry Board Inc.
(AIBI)
350 West Mart Center Drive,
suite 690
Chicago, IL 60654
www.aibi.com
(312) 836-1041
Fashion industry
organization

Craft and Hobby
Association
319 East 54th Street
Elmwood Park, NJ 07407
www.craftandhobby.org
(201) 835-1200
International not-for-profit
trade organization

Business Associations/
Organizations
American Woman's
Economic Development
Corporation (AWED)
216 East 45th Street,
10th floor
New York, NY 10017
www.awed.org
(917) 368-6100

Business Networking
International
45 College Commerce Way
Upland, CA 91786
www.bni.com
(800) 825-8286

Forté Foundation
9600 Escarpment
Suite 745 PMB 72
Austin, TX 78749
(512) 535-5157
www.fortefoundation.org
Consortium of corporations
and business schools that
serve to educate and direct
women toward leadership
roles in business

Home Based Working Moms
PO Box 1628
Spring, TX 77383
(281) 350-4390
www.hbwm.com
Online community and
professional association for
moms working at home

National Association of
Child Care Resource &
Referral Agencies
3101 Wilson Boulevard,
Suite 350
Arlington, VA 22201
(703) 341-4100
www.naccrra.org

National Association of
Female Executives (NAFE)
260 Madison Avenue,
3rd floor
New York, NY 10016
www.nafe.com
(800) 927-6233

National Association For
Moms In Business
P.O. Box 50008
Henderson, NV 89016
(571) 303-9368
www.mibn.org or www.
nafmib.org
Association representing
entrepreneur, executive, and
CEO moms

National Association of
Women Business Owners
8405 Greensboro Drive,
suite 800
McLean, VA 22102
www.nawbo.org
(800) 55-NAWBO
Advocacy and professional
membership organization

Online Women's Business
Centers
Small Business
Administration
409 Third Street SW,
6th Floor
Washington, D.C. 20416
www.onlinewbc.gov
(202) 205-6673
Part of the SBA's
Entrepreneurial
Development's network of
services

SCORE: Counselors to
America's Small Business
409 Third Street SW,
6th floor
Washington, D.C. 20024
www.score.org
(800) 634-0245
Free small business advice;
SBA partner

Small Business
Administration
409 Third Street SW
Washington, D.C. 20416
www.sba.gov
(800) U-ASK-SBA

Springboard Enterprises
2100 Foxhall Road NW
Washington, D.C. 20007
(202) 242-6282
www.springboardenterprises
.org
A nonprofit organization
dedicated to accelerating
women's access to the equity
markets

Volunteer Lawyers for the
Arts
The Paley Building
1 East 53rd Street, 6th Floor
New York, NY 10022
212 319-ARTS (2787) ext. 1
www.vlany.org
New York-based organization
providing legal aid and
resources to artists.

WIBO (Workshop in
Business Opportunities)
220 East 23rd Street,
room 309
New York, NY, 10010
www.wibo.org
(212) 684-0854
Nonprofit corporation
enabling budding
entrepreneurs in underserved
communities to start,
operate, and build successful
businesses

Women's Chamber of
Commerce
1201 Pennsylvania Avenue
NW, suite 300
Washington, D.C. 20004
www.sblink.us/html/uswcc.
aspx
(888) 41-USWCC

Women's Venture Fund
240 West 35th Street,
suite 201
New York, NY 10001
www.womensventurefund
.org
(212) 563-0499
Nonprofit organization
providing capital and
mentorship to minority
women entrepreneurs

Books

*33 Million People in the Room:
How to Create, Influence, and
Run a Successful Business with
Social Networking,* Juliette
Powell, Financial Times
Press

Crafting a Business, Kathie
Fitzgerald, Hearst Books

Crafting as a Business, Wendy
Rosen, The Rosen Group

*Good to Great: Why Some
Companies Make the Leap
. . . and Others Don't,* Jim
Collins, HarperCollins
Publishers Inc.

Making a Living in Crafts,
Donald A. Clark, Lark
Books

*Purple Cow: Transform Your
Business by Being Remarkable,*
Seth Godin, Penguin Group
(USA) Inc.

*The Art of Possibility,
Transforming Professional
and Personal Life,* Rosamund
Stone Zander and Benjamin
Zander, Harvard Business
School Press

*The Artist's Way, A Spiritual
Path to Higher Creativity,*
Julia Cameron, Penguin
Group (USA) Inc.

*The Business of Bliss: How to
Profit from Doing What You
Love,* Janet Allon and the
editors of *Victoria Magazine,*
Hearst Books

*The Do-It-Yourself Business
Book,* Gustav Berle, John
Wiley & Sons

*The E-Factor: Building a
24/7, Customer-Centric,
Electronic Business for the
Internet Age,* Martin T.
Focazio, AMACON

*The Entrepreneurial Mom:
Managing for Success in Your
Home and Your Business,*
Mary E. Davis, Turner

*The Girl's Guide to Starting
Your Own Business: Candid
Advice, Frank Talk, and
True Stories for the Successful
Entrepreneur,* Caitlin
Friedman and Kimberly Yorio,
HarperCollins Publishers Inc.

*Ladies Who Launch: An
Innovative Program that Will
Help You Get Your Dreams
Off the Ground,* Victoria
Colligan, Beth Schoenfeldt,
and Amy Swift, St. Martin's
Press

*Mommy Millionaire: How
I Turned My Kitchen Table
Idea into a Million Dollars and
How You Can, Too!,* Kim
Lavine, St. Martin's Press

*Mompreneurs: A Mother's
Practical Step by Step Guide
to Work at Home Success,*
Patricia Cobe and Ellen H.
Parlapiano, Perigee

*A Shop of One's Own:
Women Who Turned the
Dream into Reality,* Rachel
Epstein, Hearst Books

*Turn Your Passion Into
Profits: How to Start the
Business of Your Dreams,*
Janet Allon and the editors
of *Victoria Magazine,* Hearst
Books

*Working Mother's Guide to
Life: Strategies, Secrets, and
Solutions,* Linda Mason,
Three Rivers Press

*You Can Do It!: The Merit
Badge Handbook for Grown-
up Girls,* Lauren Catuzzi
Grandcolas, Chronicle
Books

Magazines

Accessories Magazine
185 Madison Avenue,
5th floor
New York, NY 10016
(212) 686-4412
www.accessoriesmagazine.
com

Country Living
300 West 57th Street
New York, NY, 10019
www.countryliving.com

The Crafts Report
100 Rogers Road
Wilmington, DE 19801
(800) 777-7098
www.craftsreport.com

Enterprising Women
1135 Kildaire Farm Road,
suite 200
Cary, NC 27511
(919) 362-9898
www.enterprisingwomen.
com

Entrepreneur
Entrepreneur Media Inc.
2445 McCabe Way,
suite 400
Irvine, CA 92614
(949) 261-2325
www.entrepreneur.com

Inc.
7 World Trade Center
New York, NY 10007
(212) 389-5377
www.inc.com

Niche
3000 Chestnut Avenue #300
Baltimore, MD 21211
(410) 889-3093, www.
nichemag.com

Sunshine Artist
Palm House Publishing
4075 L.B. McLeod Road,
suite E,
Orlando, FL 32811
(800) 597-2573
www.sunshineartist.com

Working Mother
Bonnier Corporation
2 Park Avenue, 10th Floor
New York, NY 10016
(212) 779-5110
www.workingmother.com

Shows/Events
American Art Marketing
P.O. Box 480
Slate Hill, NY 10973
www.americancraftmarketing
.com
(800) 834-9437
Organizers of the
MasterWorks Art and
Design Fair at Hancock
Shaker Village

American Craft Council
72 Spring Street, 6th floor
New York, NY 10012
(800) 836-3470
www.craftcouncil.org

AMC, Inc. /
AMERICASMART®-
ATLANTA
240 Peachtree Street, NW,
suite 2200

Atlanta, GA 30303
www.americasmart.com
(404) 220-3000
Organizers of the Atlanta
International Gift & Home
Furnishings Market

GLM Shows/George Little
Management, LLC
10 Bank Street
White Plains, NY 10606
www.glmshows.com
(914) 421-3200
Organizers of the National
Stationary Show and other
wholesale gift shows

Stella Show Management
151 West 25th Street, suite 2
New York, NY 10001
www.stellashows.com
(212) 255-0020; fax: (212)
255-0002
Antiques, art, and
collectibles

The Rosen Group
3000 Chestnut Avenue,
suite 304
Baltimore, MD 21211
http://www.americancraft.com/
(410) 889-2933
Organizers of the Buyers
Market of American Craft—
Philadelphia

SOFA
The International
Exhibition of Sculptural
Objects and Functional Art,
New York and Chicago
http://www.sofaexpo.com
info@sofaexpo.com
(800) 563-7632 or (773)
506-8860

Wendy Shows
P.O. Box 707
Rye, NY 10580
www.wendyshows.com
(914) 698-3442
Organizer of some of the
Park Avenue Seventh
Regiment Armory shows

Renegade Craft Fair
(Brooklyn, Chicago, Los
Angeles, San Francisco)
www.renegadecraft.com

Web Sites

Another Girl At Play
www.anothergirlatplay.com
Web site and discussion list
on fostering creativity

BlueSuitMom
www.bluesuitmom.com
Advice to help executive
working moms balance work
and family

Create Your Dreams
www.createyourdreamsgrant
.com
Information about grant
offered to women business
owners by the National
Association for Moms in
Business

Digital Women
www.digital-women.com
Provides small-business tools
for women entrepreneurs,
including grant information

Etsy
www.etsy.com
Site for buying and selling
crafts and artwork and for
community networking

eWomenNetwork
www.ewomennetwork.com
Networking site that
connects women and
promotes their businesses

HomeWorkingMom
www.homeworkingmom.com
Provides basic information
and tips for mothers working
at home

Ladies Who Launch
www.ladieswholaunch.com
Web site, e-mail newsletter,
and one-day conferences on
starting your own business

Make Mine Pink
www.makeminepink.com
Business networking,
community, and boutique
sales platform for women

Market Research.com
www.marketresearch.com
A continuously updated
collection of market research

MillionaireMoms
www.millionairemom.com
Social networking
and resource site for
entrepreneurial women

The Mom Pack
www.mompack.com
Network of mothers in
business working together to
build their businesses

Mommy Tracked
www.mommytracked.com
Site offering working
moms news, advice, and
information to manage busy
lives

Mompreneurs Online
www.mompreneursonline
.com
Offers articles, forums, blogs,
and products for work-at-
home moms

Mom's Buzz
www.themomsbuzz.com
Tips for busy moms

Pink
www.pinkmagazine.com
Resources, community, and
daily e-newsletter for women
in business

The Switchboards
theswitchboards.com
Networking site, connecting
creative women in business

Traditional Folk Art
www.traditionalfolkart.com
Features artists and crafts,
show listings

WomanOwned
www.womanowned.com
Business networks for
women

Women@Work Network
www.womenatwork.com
Offers advice, resources, and networking forums for working women through all life stages

WomenEntrepreneur
womenentrepreneur.com
Online edition of *Entrepreneur* magazine,

with articles and information specifically for businesswomen

Work at Home Magazine
www.wahm.com
Online magazine for work-at-home moms

Work it, Mom!
www.workitmom.com

Blogs, resources, and community for working moms

Working Moms Refuge
www.momsrefuge.com
Networking site offering discussion and advice to working mothers and business owners

DISCARD

Photography Credits

Unless noted, photos were provided by the profiled women.

AllerGale Design: 95, 97; Burcu Avsar: 73 top, 81 top; Staci Bailey Photography: 94; Christopher Bain: 50; Eric Bauer: 21; Ryan Benyi: 7 bottom right, 9, 10, 11 top, 14, 156 top left; Justin Bernhaut: 114; Darryl Bernstein: 99 bottom, 101 top, 157 bottom left; Brad Bodwell: 6 bottom left, 119, 123; Bunny Byrne: 78, 79 bottom; Kristie Cromie/L Photographie: 7 bottom middle, 144, 149; Miki Duisterhof: 1 right, 53, 55, 83, 85 top left and right, 86-87, 98, 156 top middle and right; Stacey Forsyth: 6 top right, 80; Don Freeman: 135; Jarvis M. Freymann: 112; Saxton Freymann: 107-108, 109 (child portraits), 110-111; Philip Friedman/ Studio D: 68 bottom; Thayer Allyson Gowdy: 49 bottom, 96; Ann Graf: 17 top; John Granen: 7 bottom left, 26, 27 bottom, 28 top left, 47, 48 top left and bottom right, 51, 157 top middle; James S. Greene: 11 bottom; Ryan Heffernan: 84, 85 bottom left and right, 156 bottom middle; Aimée Herring: 37-39, 57-61, 156 bottom right; Hannah Huffman: 34, 36; Susan Jackson: 147 top right and left,

156 center; Ray Kachatorian: 46; Jennifer Krough: 120-122; Courtesy of The Land of Nod: 117 both photos; Kathy Landman: 141, 142 top and bottom; Jesica Leigh: 79 top, 81 bottom right; Debra McClinton: 49 top; Ellen McDermott: 125, 126; Tasha McKelvey: 1 left, 6 middle left, 88-90, 92-93, 157 bottom middle; Brett McNeill Photography: 40; Meenophoto.com: 32; James Merrell: 132 bottom right; Keith Scott Morton: 6 top middle, 105 top left and right, 157 top left; Mountain Top Photography/www.mtpimages.com: 152, 155; Scott Paulus: 16, 19; Bergen Pierson: 41; Michael Priest: 6 middle right, 140; Kathy Quirk-Syvertsen: 43-44; Robert Rausch/GAS Studio: 7 top left, 69, 70 top left; Lara Robby/Studio D: 63, 109 left; Stephanie Schamban: 66, 67, 68 top, 70 top right, 70 bottom left and right; Christi Sisk/Digital Escape Studio: 64-65; Laurie Smith: 52, 54, 56; Juliana Thomas Photography: 138 middle and bottom, 139; Jonny Valiant: 103, 105 bottom left and right; Jason Varney: 136; Mitchell Walker: 6 center; David White: 1 middle, 27 top, 28 top right, 28 bottom photos, 29-31; Steve Wienke: 113, 115-116, 118, 156 middle right.

Index

Accountant questions, 170

Allison-Stroud, Diane, 8–13, 160, 169, 173, 175, 176–177, 178, 180, 184

Balancing act. *See also* Space and boundaries; Work–family balance

business and pleasure, 58

employment and ownership, 63

family in company, 125

family priority, 15, 22, 47, 67, 84, 99, 108, 131, 137, 141. *See also* work and home

health and prosperity, 73

interruptions and routine, 104

laughter and balance, 33

multiple roles and perfection, 10

scheduling, 22

work and home, 27, 38, 54, 89, 95, 114, 120, 145, 151. *See also* family priority

work space and home, 43, 79

Barickman, Amy, 98–102, 165, 169, 178, 179, 184

Benefits and challenges, preparing for, 159–161

Bodwell, Vicki Mote, 119–123, 174–175, 184

Business, defining, 158–159

Business plan, 163–166

checklist, 164

feedback on, 165–166

five essentials for, 166

inside track on, 165

researching before creating, 163–164

writing and rewriting, 164–165

Chapman, Heidi, 37–41, 165, 166, 184

Chung, Saras, 144–149, 161, 168–169, 172, 177, 178

Clark, Meredith, 32–36, 161, 165, 172–174, 184

Craig, Ann Marie, 14–19, 175, 181, 184

Credit cards, financing with, 167

Defining business, 158–159

Family. *See also* Balancing act; Work–family balance

carving out time for, 177–179

talking to about business ideas, 162

vacations and, 25, 55, 62, 92, 102, 122–123, 179

Financing, 167–170

building business slowly and, 168–169

checklist, 168

creative approach, 168–169

credit cards, 167

forecasts, 165

inside track on, 169

investors, 167–168

loans, 167

questions to ask accountant, 170

researching needs and options, 164

Galison, Mia, 107–112, 179, 184

Getting started. *See also* Business plan

defining business, 158–159

first steps, 158–162

inside track on, 160–161

preparing for benefits/ challenges, 159–161

talking to family about, 161–162

Greenwood, Monique, 136–139, 162, 172, 177, 179, 180–181, 184

Grey, Amy, 150–155, 161, 182, 184

Haupt, Debbie, 42–45, 173, 179, 181–182, 184

Help

expert sources, 164

from other women, 183. *See also* Inside track

resources, 184–190

How kids see it

ages to 9, 30, 60, 154

ages 10 to 15, 24, 35, 50, 76, 92, 110, 118, 123, 135

ages 16 to 20, 64, 143

ages 21 to 30, 12, 18, 40, 44, 56

In-home businesses, 171–172

Inside track

on business plan, 165

on financing, 169

on getting started, 160–161

on space and boundaries, 173

on staying on track, 182

on work–family balance, 178

Investors, 167–168

Keegan, Monique, 130–135, 182, 184

Kids. *See* "Oh no they didn't!" experiences; How kids see it; Work–family balance

Kim, Maryellen, 88–93, 161, 165, 169, 183, 184

Lenfestey, Laurie, 83–87, 161, 177, 184

List, Jennifer, 21–25, 160, 173, 184

Loans, 167

Location. *See* Space and boundaries

Malakasis, Tasia, 66–71, 160, 178, 182, 184

Market research, 163–164

McCollum, Haile, 78–82, 184

McPherson, Rachel, 140–143, 158–159, 160, 178–179, 182, 184

Mentor directory, 184–185

Me time, 181–183

Muzyka, Zhena, 72–77, 161, 181, 184

O'Connor, Jen, 57–61, 161, 173, 178, 184

"Oh no they didn't!" experiences
basket-hat cutie, 146
cherry picker/cherry wearer, 153
child entrepreneurs, 29
color confusion, 11, 127
diaper duty, 48
face-cream butter, 65
food fights and firing, 55
green tea and eggs, 75
packing-peanut fun, 34
playing 'house' and dad cooking, 45
potty interruptions, 60, 117

Owens, Yolanda, 62–65, 158, 169, 181, 182, 184

Paganelli, Jennifer, 103–106, 184

Pitfalls & triumphs, 16, 23, 80, 111, 121, 138

Profiles of success (artisans)
chandeliers and sconces, 32–36
children's clothing/ accessories, 21–25
felted home and baby accessories, 26–31
handcrafted soaps, 14–19
handmade game boards, 8–13

Profiles of success (designer/ producers)
artisan goat cheese, 66–71
fabric-arts supplies, 98–102
greeting cards and wrapping paper, 94–97

handcrafted home/fashion accessories, 88–93
handcrafted journals, frames, cards, jewelry, 83–87
home and apparel textiles/ accessories, 103–106
kids' accessories and toys, 113–118, 119–123
kids' games, activities, gifts, 107–112
organic, fair-trade teas, 72–77
personalized gifts/ stationery, 78–82
skin care products, 62–65

Profiles of success (service providers)
bed & breakfast, 136–139
business support for female artisans, 144–149
home/landscape design, construction, and accessories, 130–135
interior design and home accessories, 124–129
produce for needy, 150–155
therapy dog services, 140–143

Profiles of success (shop owners/event producers)
antiques and more, 37–41, 42–45, 46–51
bakery and café, 52–56
folk-artists' representative, 57–61

Raphael, Carrie, 124–129, 160, 184

Rather, Rebecca, 52–56, 184

Research, 163–164

Resources, 184–190

Schriber, Barbara, 94–97, 159, 169, 182, 185

Space and boundaries, 171–175
balancing, 43, 79
in-home businesses, 171–172

inside track on, 173
outside-of-home businesses, 174–175
staff in home, 172–174

Staying on track. See also Help
inside track on, 182
as lessons in disguise, 180–181
me time and, 181–183
preparing for challenges and, 159–161

Thompson, Serena, 46–51, 165, 178, 185

Vacations, 25, 55, 62, 92, 102, 122–123, 179

Waddington, Stacy, 21–25, 184

White, Betz, 26–31, 179, 182, 185

Wienke, Libby, 113–118, 168, 172, 181, 182, 183, 185

Work–family balance, 176–179. See also Balancing act
carving out family time, 177–179
inside track on, 178
staying focused, 177
working around family, 176–177

Work space. See Space and boundaries